GUATEMALA
GETTING AWAY WITH MURDER

August 1991

An
Americas Watch
and
Physicians for Human Rights
Report

Americas Watch
485 Fifth Avenue
Third Floor
New York, NY 10017-6104
TEL: 212-972-8400
FAX: 212-972-0905

Physicians for Human Rights
58 Day Street
Suite 202
Somerville, MA 02144
TEL: 617-623-1930
FAX: 617-623-7234

ISBN: 1-56432-024-3.
Library of Congress Catalog Card Number: 91-73249.
Cover design by: Charlotte Staub

Americas Watch was established in 1981 to monitor and promote the observance of internationally recognized human rights. Americas Watch is one of the five regional Committees of Human Rights Watch. The Chair of Americas Watch is Peter D. Bell; Vice Chairs, Stephen L. Kass and Marina Pinto Kaufman; Executive Director, Juan E. Méndez.

Human Rights Watch is composed of the five Watch Committees -- Africa Watch, Americas Watch, Asia Watch, Helsinki Watch and Middle East Watch -- and the Fund for Free Expression. Its Chair is Robert L. Bernstein; Vice Chair, Adrian W. DeWind; Executive Director, Aryeh Neier; Deputy Director, Kenneth Roth; Washington Director, Holly J. Burkhalter; California Director, Ellen Lutz; Press Director, Susan Osnos; Counsel, Jemera Rone.

Physicians for Human Rights (PHR) is a national organization of health professionals whose goal is to bring the skills of the medical profession to the protection of human rights.

Americas Watch
485 Fifth Avenue
Third Floor
New York, NY 10017-6104
TEL: 212-972-8400
FAX: 212-972-0905
Email (PeaceNet):
"hrwatchnyc"

1522 K Street, NW
Suite 910
Washington, DC 20005
TEL: 212-371-6592
FAX: 212-371-0124
Email (PeaceNet):
"hrwatchdc"

Physicians for Human Rights
58 Day Street
Suite 202
Somerville, MA 02144
TEL: 617-623-7234
FAX: 617-623-7234

"If anyone wanted to commit murder and get away with it, they should come to Guatemala."

--Clyde Collins Snow
December 10, 1990

.

TABLE OF CONTENTS

ACKNOWLEDGMENTS

I. INTRODUCTION AND SUMMARY OF CONCERNS 1
    A. National Mechanisms for Investigating Abuses 5
    B. Non-governmental Human Rights Monitors 11
    C. Summary of Concerns 13

II. THE MEDICOLEGAL SYSTEM IN GUATEMALA 17
    A. Background 17
    B. Guatemala's Death Investigation System 20

III. DISAPPEARANCES, TORTURE, AND EXTRAJUDICIAL
     KILLINGS 29
     A. Sebastián Velásquez Mejía, Chunimá 32
     B. María Mejía, Parraxtut 36
     C. Myrna Elizabeth Mack Chang 39
     D. Torture and Murder of Street Children 45

IV. THE MASSACRE AT SANTIAGO ATITLAN 53

V. DIGGING UP THE PAST: THE GRAVES AT SAN ANTONIO
    SINACHE 65
    A. Disinterment and Analysis of Skeletal Remains 69
    B. Manuel Tiniguar Chitic 71
    C. Sebastián Cos Morales and Pedro Tiniguar Turquiz .. 73
    D. Future Exhumations 75

VI. THE ROLE OF THE UNITED STATES 77

VII. OBSERVATIONS AND RECOMMENDATIONS 81
     A. Military and Economic Aid 81
     B. Police Training 81
     C. Other Assistance for Medicolegal Investigations 82
     D. The Medicolegal System 82
     E. Exhumantions and Guatemala's Disappeared 83
     F. Investigations and Political Will 84
     G. The Protection of Human Rights Monitors 85

APPENDICES 87
   A. Forensic Investigative Report Re: Myrna Elizabeth
       Mack Chang
   B. Human Skeletal Remains Exhumed From San Antonio de
       Sinaché, Guatemala on January 9, 1991
   C. Minnesota Protocol I -- Model Autopsy Protocol
   D. Minnesota Protocol II -- Model Protocol for Disinterment
       and Analysis of Skeletal Remains
   E. Human Rights Monitors Killed or Disappeared in Guatemala

ACKNOWLEDGMENTS

This report was written by Anne Manuel, Associate Director of Americas Watch, and Eric Stover, a freelance writer and consultant to Human Rights Watch and Physicians for Human Rights (PHR). A mission including the authors, Dr. Robert H. Kirschner, the Deputy Chief Medical Examiner for Cook Country, Illinois; and forensic anthropologist Clyde Collins Snow traveled to Guatemala in December 1990. Snow and Stover returned for a second mission in January 1991. Attorney Emily Yozell laid the groundwork for our first visit and provided valuable research assistance and translation. Patricia Sinay and Louise Pisano Simone assisted in the production of this report.

We are grateful to several judges, forensic doctors, and their assistants, who provided useful insight and information. Our greatest debt of gratitude is owed to Guatemala's growing community of human rights activists. In particular we would like to thank the Human Rights Office of the Archdiocese of Guatemala, the Council of Ethnic Communities "We Are All Equal" (CERJ), the Mutual Support Group for the Appearance Alive of Our Relatives (GAM), the Office of Human Rights/Human Life of the Diocese of Sololá, and Casa Alianza. Their work and the work of other human rights monitors in Guatemala provides us with tremendous inspiration and gives us hope that Guatemala may some day emerge from the human rights nightmare it has experienced for many decades.

Sadly, those people who work inside Guatemala to improve human rights face persecution and danger each day. (The final appendix to this report lists 27 human rights activists killed or disappeared in Guatemala since 1974.) Indeed, two human rights activists we met with in December 1990 have been the victims of violence since our visit. CERJ members Diego Perebal León and Manuel Perebal Morales were shot on February 17, 1991 (see Chapter III). Perebal Morales perished in the attack and Perebal León was severely wounded and is now confined to a wheelchair. Their father, CERJ member Juan Perebal Xirúm, also died in the shooting. Two more CERJ members have been murdered in recent months. The persecution of human rights activists remains the most discouraging aspect of the very bleak human rights situation in Guatemala today.

I. INTRODUCTION

Ever since a U.S.-managed military coup overthrew a reformist, democratic government in 1954, Guatemala has been known as a place where soldiers and policemen, untrammeled by legal restraints of any kind, torture and murder in the name of anticommunism. In 1985, the military allowed the election of a civilian government, and the next year Christian Democrat Vinicio Cerezo Arévalo took office promising to end military impunity and build the foundations of democratic governance.[1]

Cerezo faced two fundamental human rights problems: grappling with the violent past and stopping ongoing abuses. While civilian governments in Argentina, Bolivia, and Chile have sought an accounting for the gross violations of human rights committed by previous military regimes, the Cerezo government avoided the issue. On the campaign trail in 1985, Cerezo said: "We are not going to be able to investigate the past. We would have to put the entire army in jail."[2] Thus tens of thousands of extrajudicial executions and disappearances[3] have never been investigated and those responsible for these crimes remain in command of the military. Thousands of relatives still do not know the fate of loved ones who disappeared after being seized by the security forces, and the countryside is strewn with the unmarked graves of their victims.

Nor have Guatemala's civilian governments stopped human rights abuses. Throughout Cerezo's five-year term, the security forces continued to kill, torture, and "disappear" their perceived opponents with impunity. In late 1990, a year widely perceived as the bloodiest under the Cerezo government, the congressionally appointed Human Rights Ombudsman (*Procurador de los Derechos Humanos*) reported

---

[1] Guatemala had one civilian government between the time of the 1954 coup and the inauguration of President Cerezo in 1986. However, the 1966 – 1970 administration of President Julio César Méndez Montenegro was widely recognized as no more than a civilian face on continued military rule.

[2] Jean-Marie Simon, *Guatemala: Eternal Spring, Eternal Tyranny*, (New York: W.W. Norton & Co., 1987), p. 227.

[3] A disappearance occurs when the security forces or their agents take a victim into custody but deny holding him or her. In Guatemala, the disappeared are usually interrogated, tortured, and killed; their bodies disposed of secretly.

that 588 individuals had been the victim of extrajudicial executions over the year and that another 140 had disappeared.[4]

A new civilian president, Jorge Serrano Elías, took office on January 14, 1991. He, too, promised to punish those responsible for human rights abuses. "Hierarchies will not be able to go against the majesty of the law," Serrano pronounced at his inauguration. "He who breaks the law shall be punished without exception."[5] Yet in the first three months of 1991, the Ombudsman reported 180 extrajudicial executions and 46 disappearances, suggesting a trend for the worse. In April, May, June, and July 1991, a campaign of death threats against the leaders of unions, human rights groups, and members of the moderate-left opposition provoked a stampede into exile. In addition, a series of high-profile assassinations which appeared to have political motives shocked the country. The victims included Dinora Pérez Valdez, who had been a congressional candidate for a social democratic political grouping in the November 1990 elections; Brother Moisés Cisneros, of the Marist order; Air Force General Anacleto Maza Castellanos; Appeals Court judge Raúl Sao Villagrán; and agronomist Julio Quevedo, a member of the pastoral team of the Bishop of El Quiché province.

While some encouragement can be drawn from the January 1991 conviction of four policemen for the murder of a street child, the Serrano administration's failure to enforce more than a dozen arrest warrants against civil patrollers (who apparently enjoy army protection) for several incidents of assault, kidnapping, and murder of human rights activists in 1990 and 1991 suggests the new administration is no more capable of confronting the army over human rights abuses than was its predecessor (see Chapter III).

This report examines many of the flaws in Guatemala's system of death investigation and suggests ways in which it can be improved. Some of the more fundamental changes include upgrading the conditions and equipment in judicial morgues throughout the country, increasing the number of forensic doctors, providing forensic doctors

---

[4] The Ombudsman's figures most likely understate the problem, as they are based on press reports, which do not adequately cover rural areas, and complaints from individuals who come to the Ombudsman's office. Many Guatemalans fear reporting violations to a government agency.

[5] Speech by President Jorge Serrano Elías, as reprinted in *Foreign Broadcast Information Service Daily Report Latin America* [hereinafter *"FBIS"*], (Washington, D.C.: January 16, 1991), p. 14.

with better university training, and increasing their independence and powers of investigation. The most important improvement, however, must be undertaken by Guatemala's civilian and military leaders. They must commit themselves to investigating and punishing those responsible for violations of human rights, no matter what their position is. Until they are willing to make such a commitment, lawlessness will continue. Getting away with murder is easy in Guatemala not only because of the lack of skills, equipment, and training on the part of forensic doctors and the archaic system of death investigation under which they work, but because the entire system is subverted by the involvement of government forces in the same crimes they are supposed to investigate.

Most human rights violations are never investigated in Guatemala.[6] Our delegation studied the rare cases in which an investigation was pursued. To understand why these investigations ran aground, Americas Watch and Physicians for Human Rights sent missions to Guatemala in December 1990 and January 1991. Unlike delegations which examined various legal aspects of Guatemala's criminal justice system, we were specifically concerned with the application of medical and scientific procedures in death investigations. In addition to assessing the system in general, we examined the conduct of investigations in several specific cases of political killings, most of which took place in 1990. Our case studies include human rights monitors slain for their efforts to defend the rights of their compatriots, street children persecuted by the Guatemala City police, peaceful protesters gunned down by soldiers near the tourist mecca of Santiago Atitlán, and peasants killed on the orders of civil patrol chiefs in a highland village seven years ago. These cases represent diverse forms of persecution practiced by different elements of the state's security apparatus.

The second purpose of our visit was to offer assistance to judges and human rights investigators who are seeking to uncover and document the history of military repression in the early 1980s through exhumations of clandestine graves. Guatemala's highland provinces of El Quiché and Huehuetenango contain hundreds of unmarked graves. Within these graves are buried the victims of the military's notorious scorched earth campaigns of the early 1980s. During this period, the military swept through the countryside killing suspected

---

[6] See Washington Office on Latin America, *The Administration of Injustice: Military Accountability in Guatemala*, (Washington, D.C.: December 1989).

3

guerrilla supporters. On several occasions, entire communities were massacred. Now relatives of the victims and human rights groups in Guatemala are pressing the courts to unearth these graves for several reasons: so that their loved ones can finally receive dignified burials; so that the history of a brutal era which deeply traumatized the highland population can be recognized and officially acknowledged; and finally, so that the perpetrators of these atrocities can be tried and punished.

Americas Watch and Physicians for Human Rights selected two forensic experts -- Dr. Robert H. Kirschner and Clyde Collins Snow -- to accompany staff on our visits. Dr. Kirschner is a forensic pathologist and the Deputy Chief Medical Examiner of Cook County, Illinois. He has observed or participated in human rights investigations in Argentina, El Salvador, Kenya, Czechoslovakia, the West Bank and Gaza, South Korea, and the United States. Snow is a forensic anthropologist, a scientist who applies his knowledge of human skeletal variation to medicolegal investigations. Since 1985, Snow has trained and worked with the Argentine Forensic Anthropology Team which is identifying the skeletal remains of Argentina's "disappeared." Snow and the Argentine team have also provided assistance in human rights investigations in Bolivia, Brazil, the Philippines, Uruguay, Venezuela, and Chile.

On the first mission to Guatemala, in December 1990, Snow and Kirschner were accompanied by Anne Manuel, Associate Director of Americas Watch; Eric Stover, a freelance writer and a consultant to Physicians for Human Rights and Human Rights Watch; and attorney Emily Yozell. In January 1991, Snow and Stover returned to Guatemala to exhume two unmarked graves in the central highlands and to interview survivors of the December 1990 massacre in Santiago Atitlán.

During our visits, we met with victims of human rights abuses, their relatives, and witnesses to abuses; forensic doctors in the capital and in rural departments; firemen, whose job it is to collect bodies; judges, police officers, human rights activists, both private and governmental; lawyers, journalists, and the U.S. Ambassador. On December 12, we observed the exhumation of the body of human rights activist Sebastián Velásquez Mejía at the request of family members. Velásquez Mejía had been kidnapped two months earlier and although a body bearing his identification card had been found and buried shortly thereafter, serious doubts existed as to whether the body indeed was his. These doubts were put to rest by the exhumation. Days later, Snow and Stover conducted the first of

4

several exhumations of graves of young men killed by a local civil patrol chief in 1984 on suspicion of sympathizing with the guerrillas.

We were encouraged to find that many Guatemalan forensic doctors and judges were very interested in using the skills of their professions to investigate human rights abuses. However, their ability to do this work is greatly hindered by a lack of training and equipment and serious flaws in the medicolegal system (outlined below), in addition to the knowledge that serious efforts to investigate and prosecute human rights offenses may put their lives at grave risk. That nongovernmental human rights groups are dedicated to this effort is beyond question. We are hopeful that the international community will takes steps to nurture the efforts underway by brave individuals in Guatemala to implement the rule of law through serious investigations leading to criminal prosecutions.

A. National Mechanisms for Investigating Abuses

The Cerezo administration indicated early on that it would rely on the criminal courts to investigate and prosecute those responsible for human rights abuses. Throughout his tenure, President Cerezo resisted calls for an independent commission to investigate the fate of the disappeared. Moreover, the possibilities for bringing to trial cases from the early 1980s were limited both by the *de facto* immunity from prosecution enjoyed by the military, and by amnesty decrees passed by previous military regimes to protect themselves from justice.

Days before turning over office to President Cerezo, the military regime of General Oscar Humberto Mejía Víctores promulgated Decree Law 8-86 granting amnesty for "political crimes and related common crimes" during his administration and during the 1982–1983 rule of General Efraín Ríos Montt. An earlier amnesty covers crimes committed during the reign of General Romeo Lucas García from 1978 – 1982. It has generally been assumed that these amnesties legally eliminated the already slim possibility that members of the military could be criminally punished for atrocities committed between 1978 – 1986. Yet this assumption has never been tested by the courts and may be erroneous in the case of the 1986 law. Although the 1982 amnesty, Decree-Law No. 33-82, specifically exempted from prosecution "members of the Security Forces of the State who in fulfilling their duty participated in counter–subversion activities," the amnesty enacted in 1986 applied "to any person responsible or accused of having committed political and related common crimes during the period between March 23, 1982 and January 14, 1986." In an April 13, 1989 interview with Americas Watch, Supreme Court President Edmundo Vásquez Martínez explained that "political and related common crimes" are by definition crimes against the State, such as guerrilla insurgency or military coup attempts, not human rights violations, such as assassinations of individuals targeted for their political views.

Studying the shortcomings of the criminal justice system in Guatemala is a disheartening pursuit; at virtually every stage major obstacles to achieving justice are easily found. The system is permeated by fear, from the witnesses and relatives who dare not testify or issue a complaint for fear of retribution, to the prosecutors and judges who must think of their families when evidence leads to the army's doorstep. Corruption, although difficult to measure, is also a significant factor in a country where public officials -- from police to judges -- draw extremely low paychecks.

The most obvious reason for the judiciary's failure to prosecute human rights violators is that the police, who actually perform most of the investigative work, are themselves direct participants in assassination, torture, and disappearances. Further, the police, although nominally under the jurisdiction of the Interior Ministry, remain effectively under army control, making them unwilling to investigate cases where the army is implicated.[7] Under the new Serrano government, as under President Cerezo, the director of the National Police is an army colonel, Mario Paíz Bolaños.

The judiciary has historically been the weakest branch of government in Guatemala, and it has failed to assert itself in prosecuting human rights offenders despite a three-year training program run by Harvard University's Center for Criminal Justice and funded by the U.S. Agency for International Development. The Harvard program focussed on developing reforms in more than a dozen "model courts" in various departments. It included training in investigative techniques, efforts to improve coordination between police, prosecutors, and judges, and development of oral, public trials, instead of the written, non-public trials which characterize the Guatemalan system. Measures were suggested to reduce the

---

[7] See Americas Watch, *Closing the Space: Human Rights in Guatemala, May 1987 - October 1988*, (Washington, D.C.: November 1988), p. 20, for comment from a high-ranking police official that police investigators were unable to close investigations into hundreds of cases of disappearances that occurred between 1982 - 1987 because "they keep running into the G-2," army intelligence.

vulnerability of judges to intimidation and corruption and to improve access to the court system for indigenous residents of rural areas.[8]

In the rare cases where judges have seriously addressed political killings committed by government forces, the results have been discouraging. Since the beginning of the Cerezo administration, only one such case has actually been tried.[9] This case involved the October 1987 murder of two students at the Western University Center in the city of Quezaltenango. The students, who had participated in protests against police activities, were kidnapped by armed plainclothesmen, their bodies dumped in different parts of the country several days later. In July 1988, after unprecedented publicity and public pronouncements in favor of prosecution by senior government officials, six Guatemalan policemen, including the departmental chief of police, were tried and sentenced to the maximum penalty of thirty years for kidnapping and murder. The decision was remanded for further investigation by an appeals court in December 1988. Seven months later, a trial court reaffirmed the convictions of the police on murder charges, but for reasons which remain unknown, acquitted them on charges of kidnapping. In July 1990, a Guatemala City appeals court overturned the murder convictions and ordered the men freed.[10] The Supreme Court dismissed an appeal of the acquittal (*recurso de casación*) on procedural grounds in March 1991. A further appeal may be mounted in the future by the Attorney General's office and the non-governmental Center for the Investigation, Study, and Promotion of Human Rights (CIEPRODH). The Quezaltenango case was an exception to the general rule that political murders never get to trial.

---

[8] Written Statement of Philip Benjamin Heymann, James Barr Ames Professor of Law, Harvard Law School, at Hearing Before the Subcommittee on Western Hemisphere Affairs of the Committee on Foreign Affairs, House of Representatives, *Options for United States Policy Toward Guatemala* (Washington, D.C.: U.S. Government Printing Office, July 17, 1990), pp. 10 – 16, [hereinafter "Hearing"].

[9] Nonetheless, two cases involving the slaying by police of street children suspected of common criminal activity have been tried recently. Both cases resulted in convictions, although police were given suspended sentences in one of them. These cases are discussed in Chapter III.

[10] The case is analyzed in detail in *News From Americas Watch*, "Guatemala: Sole Conviction in Human Rights Case Overturned," (New York: August 1990).

A second case in which authorities made a serious but aborted effort to prosecute is known as the White Van Case. Beginning in early February 1988, armed plainclothesmen driving one or more white vans were seen abducting university students in Guatemala City. Several of the students were later found dead.

Later that month, then–Interior Minister Juan José Rodil announced that the "phantom van," as it had come to be called in the press, belonged to the Treasury Police and that the National Police had arrested six Treasury Police agents in connection with the abductions. The National Police conducted a fairly thorough investigation and the director reportedly presented the presiding judge with a 300–page file containing evidence implicating the Treasury Police in killings and abductions which they allegedly conducted using three white vans. On July 18, twenty–four Treasury Police agents were detained for questioning, but they were released later that month after the judge in charge of arraignment was kidnapped and interrogated for three days and his friend and advisor killed.[11] No action has been taken against the accused since they were released.

A third case, in which arrest warrants against leaders of the civil patrols for killing human rights activists have for months been ignored by the police, is discussed in Chapter III.

These were among the few cases which led to criminal prosecutions for political killings during the Cerezo Administration. No other cases progressed as far before being halted by the unseen hand that guards military and police impunity.

Upon announcing the termination of its program in Guatemala in July 1990, Harvard University professor Philip B. Heymann lamented the lack of will on the part of senior military and civilian authorities to prosecute those responsible for grave violations of human rights. In testimony before the Western Hemisphere Affairs Subcommittee of the Foreign Affairs Committee of the U.S. House of Representatives, Heymann described the Guatemalan authorities' response to a string of murders of students at the University of San Carlos in August and September of 1989:[12]

---

[11] See Americas Watch, *Closing the Space*, p. 28 – 30.

[12] See *News from Americas Watch*, "Guatemala: Renewed Violence Against Students," (New York: October 1989); and Americas Watch, *Messengers of Death: Human Rights in Guatemala*, (New York: March 1990), pp. 13 – 20.

The United States and other Western nations had poured millions of dollars into the training of judges, prosecutors and police. It was too late in the day for the highest authorities in Guatemala to claim that the incompetence of the criminal justice system prevented effective investigation. That was simply no longer true. Accordingly, we developed a list of the steps that Western nations had taken when confronted with a spate of terrorist killings of the sort that was occurring in Guatemala. They are familiar steps -- some as easy as an offer of rewards for information or an offer of anonymity to informers. I proposed them orally to the Minister of Defense. I believe the United States Embassy sent its own version to the President and the Minister of Government....I told then Minister of Defense [Héctor Alejandro] Gramajo that Harvard would not stay if there was no clear sign of a willingness to investigate such political terrorism.

To the best of my knowledge nothing was done, not the slightest effort was made, to mount a vigorous and determined investigation of the student killings.[13]

One of the few promising developments which accompanied the advent of civilian government was the establishment of the position of the Human Rights Ombudsman, charged with investigating and publicly reporting on human rights violations and promoting remedies. The Ombudsman has an office in Guatemala City and in most rural departments. Although the 1986 law creating the office gives it broad investigatory powers, the first Ombudsman named by the Congress led the office into insignificance and disrepute.[14] His resignation in October 1989, however, paved the way for the naming of the current Ombudsman, Ramiro de León Carpio, who has energetically pushed human rights into the forefront of public debate. Under its new leadership, the Ombudsman's office has made a commendable effort to track the most serious abuses nationwide, releasing statistics every few months on political killings and disappearances, and conducting in-depth investigations into selected cases. In addition, the Ombudsman and his staff have traveled to remote areas in an effort to offer protection to victims of human rights violations and their relatives. On two occasions in 1990 -- once in the hamlet of

---

[13] Hearing, pp. 17 - 18.

[14] See Americas Watch, *Closing the Space*, pp. 58 - 60.

Parraxtut and once in Chunimá, in El Quiché province --- civil patrollers attacked adjunct ombudsman César Alvarez Guadamuz as he escorted villagers forced to flee their communities because of death threats back to their homes.[15]

With assistance from the governments of West Germany and the United States, the Ombudsman's office plans to develop a well-trained investigatory staff and several forensic laboratories -- including a fingerprint laboratory, a medical examiner's office, a photography department, and a graphology section -- that will conduct investigations parallel to those of the police.[16] Breaking the police monopoly on criminal investigations could be a major breakthrough in Guatemala's justice system. Yet how the courts will handle evidence collected by the Ombudsman's office, especially if it conflicts with that provided by the police, remains to be seen.

The major limitation to the effectiveness of the Ombudsman's office is the fact that its involvement in a case ends once a formal complaint is filed in court. From then on, the case is handled by the Attorney General's office, which is understaffed and has failed to aggressively prosecute such cases. One prosecutor in the Attorney General's office apologetically told our delegation why he and his colleagues pursue such cases only mechanically. "It's difficult work

---

[15] In both cases the villagers decided not to stay, based on the hostile reception they were afforded by the patrols. The adjunct ombudsman was later able to escort the villagers back to their homes in Parraxtut and Chunimá, although three of the Chunimá villagers -- including two interviewed by our delegation -- were shot by the same civil patrollers who had threatened them in February 1991. Two perished in the attack and a third was left paralyzed. The next month, after the police failed to arrest the Chunimá patrollers responsible for the murders, the adjunct ombudsman evacuated fifteen villagers from Chunimá in recognition that their safety could not be guaranteed in their community. See *News From Americas Watch*, "Guatemala: Army Campaign Against Rights Activists Intensifies," (New York: May 1990), pp. 5 - 6; *News From Americas Watch*, "Guatemala: Rights Abuses Escalate As Elections Near," (New York: November 8, 1990), pp. 8 - 9; and *News From Americas Watch*, "Guatemala: Slaying of Rights Activists, Impunity Prevail Under New Government," (New York: April 14, 1991).

[16] Andres Oppenheimer, "Guatemala's human rights office looks to increase impact," *The Miami Herald*, September 15, 1990; and Americas Watch and PHR interview with Human Rights Ombudsman Ramiro de León Carpio and staff, December 13, 1990.

because the police are against you, the army is against you and you don't get life insurance," he said.

Months after our visits, the new government acceded to a longstanding request by human rights activists to establish an investigative commission to establish the fate of tens of thousands of Guatemalans who have disappeared at the hands of the security forces. The commission will be composed of Human Rights Ombudsman de León Carpio and his staff. Discouraged that the commission will not have broader participation, the Mutual Support Group for the Appearance Alive of Our Relatives (GAM) –– a domestic human rights group –– is pressing for legislation that would create a parallel commission with representatives of the Attorney General's office, the Congress, the Supreme Court, and human rights groups. While it is too early to evaluate the potential effectiveness of either commission, we are encouraged to see movement on this crucial issue and urge the authorities to offer investigators their full cooperation. We would also urge that all exhumations of the disappeared be carried out not only for identification purposes, but also to determine the cause and manner of death.

B. Non–governmental Human Rights Monitors

Several non–governmental human rights groups monitor political killings, disappearances, and torture, but their ability to conduct investigations has been sharply proscribed by fierce repression, including the murder or disappearance of 23 rights monitors since 1986. Even so, domestic human rights groups have made a tremendous contribution towards increasing public awareness and education on human rights.

The oldest of these groups is the Mutual Support Group (GAM), an association of relatives of the disappeared formed in 1984. The GAM undertakes a broad range of support and advocacy activities on behalf of relatives of the tens of thousands of Guatemalans who have disappeared at the hands of the security forces.[17]

Another group, the Center for Investigation, Study, and Promotion of Human Rights (CIEPRODH), was established in Guatemala City in 1987 and has since a extended to other departments. The Center conducts seminars on human rights topics, produces bulletins and

---

[17] See Americas Watch, *Guatemala: The Group for Mutual Support*, (New York: 1985).

statistics on abuses based on press reports and complaints by individuals who come to its offices, and provides legal assistance to victims.

The Council of Ethnic Communities "We Are All Equal" (CERJ), formed in 1988, seeks above all to assist peasants who wish to resign from civil patrol duty; however, as many of its members have come under attack by the military and its agents, the CERJ has increasingly become involved in documenting individual cases of abuse.[18]

The Human Rights Office of the Archdiocese of Guatemala, which opened in January 1990, has carried out several on site investigations over the course of the year and aspires to develop, through an inter-diocesan network, the capacity to monitor human rights conditions systematically across the nation. The Archbishop's office also provides legal services to victims and relatives of victims of human rights abuses.

Finally, the Confederation of Religious of Guatemala (CONFREGUA) opened a human rights office in February 1990 which provides legal assistance as well as tracking human rights violations.

Guatemala may be the country in the world where the individuals who work to improve human rights conditions are at the greatest risk of themselves becoming victims of human rights abuses. In the Human Rights Watch annual survey of persecution of human rights activists around the world in 1990, Guatemala received the ignominious distinction of being the country where the greatest number of monitors had been murdered or disappeared.[19]

Twenty-seven human rights activists have been killed or disappeared since 1974, when the first efforts were made to establish domestic human rights groups (see Appendix E). All but four of those were slain or disappeared since civilian government was established in 1986, a fact which underlines the degree to which the political opening which accompanied the transition to elected government has been accompanied by repression of those taking advantage of the new space. Eight monitors were killed and two disappeared in 1990. In the first six months of this year, four more have been slain and one

---

[18] See Americas Watch, *Persecuting Human Rights Monitors: The CERJ in Guatemala*, (New York: May 1989).

[19] Human Rights Watch, *The Persecution of Human Rights Monitors, December 1989 to December 1990, A Worldwide Survey*, (New York: December 1990), p. 2.

disappeared, all of them members of the Quiché-based CERJ. Many other monitors have received death threats in recent months, including Amílcar Méndez Urízar, the President of the CERJ, Nineth de García, President of the GAM, and Rosalina Tuyuc, the National Coordinating Body of Guatemalan Widows (CONAVIGUA).

Most of the recent killings of human rights activists in rural areas are believed to be the work of local civil patrol chiefs (see Chapter III), themselves acting out a script written by the army. Since January 1989, the army has engaged in a massive propaganda campaign in the highland departments where the CERJ and GAM have been active, to publicly link human rights activities with subversion. This campaign has included army visits to scores of communities, mostly in the southern part of El Quiché department, where meetings were held to explain that human rights and communism were synonymous. These accusations bear a special significance in Guatemala, where the army destroyed hundreds of villages and massacred thousands of peasants on the suspicion that they sympathized or supported the nation's leftist guerrillas. That the army has specifically instructed patrollers to attack human rights monitors has been documented in several cases.[20] In other cases, the patrollers may simply be responding to the army's general dictum that human rights equals subversion, which the patrollers are duty-bound to combat.

Because the work of human rights monitors is fundamental to the establishment of respect for human rights in Guatemala, we consider the violent campaign against them to be the most serious human rights problem in Guatemala today. Several of the cases analyzed in this report concern investigations into the murder of human rights activists.

C. Summary of Concerns

Americas Watch and Physicians for Human Rights have the following concerns regarding the criminal and medicolegal investigation of gross violations of human rights in Guatemala:

● **Virtually nothing has been done to investigate or punish those responsible for tens of thousands of cases of torture, murder and disappearance committed by the military, police, and civil patrols in Guatemala during the long years of military**

---

[20] See *News From Americas Watch*, "Guatemala: Army Campaign Against Rights Activists Intensifies," May 1990; and Human Rights Watch, *World Report 1990*, (New York: January 1991), pp. 175 – 178.

government which ended in 1986. The Cerezo government evaded its responsibility to provide accountability for past abuses. The Serrano government has taken a long overdue step in this direction, by authorizing the Human Rights Ombudsman to form a commission to investigate the disappearances which occurred under military rule.

● **Guatemala's highlands contain hundreds, if not thousands, of unmarked graves.** Most of them hold the victims of the military's counterinsurgency programs of the early 1980s. Military authorities have dismissed the clandestine cemeteries as the burial grounds of guerrillas killed in combat. Relatives who have sought exhumations have found their efforts obstructed by the courts. Many have been threatened with death.

● **In the first six months of the Serrano administration (January – June 1991), government forces continued to commit torture, murder, and disappearance with impunity.** Although President Serrano came into office promising to establish the rule of law, his failure to do so has been dramatically highlighted in several cases. Between May 1990 and May 1991, judges have issued more than nineteen warrants for the arrest of civil patrollers implicated in attacks, threats, kidnapping, and murder of human rights activists. Only four of those named have been detained. In the most notorious case, the former civil patrol chief of Chunimá, whose arrest was ordered but not carried out for the kidnapping and murder of a human rights activist in October 1990, later shot three more human rights monitors, leaving two of them dead and the third paralyzed. One of the deceased and the survivor were witnesses to the abduction of the patrol chief's earlier victim.

● **Police, military, and judicial investigations into human rights cases have been badly mishandled.** Particularly noteworthy are the cases of the massacre by the army of 13 Tzutujil Indians near Santiago Atitlán on December 2, 1990, and the murder of anthropologist Myrna Mack on September 11, 1990. More than a month after the massacre at Santiago Atitlán, neither the military nor the police had conducted an on site investigation, nor had the military judge in charge of the investigation interviewed any eyewitnesses. Seven months after the crime, despite the presence of hundreds of witnesses, no one has been formally charged. In the police investigation of the murder of anthropologist Myrna Mack, key

14

evidence was lost or destroyed. Although a suspect was named by the court nine months after the crime, he has not been apprehended.

• **The police, who are in charge of major portions of criminal investigations in Guatemala, continue to be responsible for many grave violations of human rights.** Some of the worst of these abuses have been directed against street children. Although nominally under civilian control, the police are effectively governed by the army, which is also responsible for many violent abuses. These factors create an inherent conflict of interest which paralyzes death investigations.

• **Guatemala's forensic doctors are deeply demoralized after decades of military rule and years of unkept civilian promises. Doctors lack modern equipment and training in forensic medicine, and they work under appalling conditions with low salaries.**

• **Guatemala's antiquated medicolegal system is in need of major reform.** Its criminal procedure code contains no provisions allowing forensic doctors to go to crime scenes. As a result, vital evidence, such as blood samples, hair, or fibers, which untrained investigators may easily overlook, are rarely, if ever, collected and properly analyzed.

• **In Guatemala, forensic doctors are only required to determine the *cause* of death (asphyxiation, loss of blood, heart attack, etc.), not the *manner* of death (homicide, suicide, natural, or accidental).** The fact that determination is left to the judge, who usually has no training in medicine, let alone forensic pathology, leaves a great possibility for misdiagnosis.

• **Although the U.S. Government has taken several positive steps in 1990, including the suspension of military aid and commercial arms sales, and the issuance of strong public statements on human rights, the Bush Administration continues to request from the Congress large amounts of security assistance.** Americas Watch and Physicians for Human Rights oppose security assistance to Guatemala as long as government forces continue to commit gross violations of human rights with impunity.

• **The criminal investigations assistance program provided by the U.S. Department of Justice to the Guatemalan police for the past five years has failed to meet its objectives.** The police continue to mishandle criminal investigations and, at the same time, continue to commit human rights abuses. Americas Watch and Physicians for Human Rights oppose further assistance to the police until there is firm evidence that they have begun to conduct serious investigations of crimes, including those committed by the authorities. Further, Americas Watch and Physicians for Human Rights oppose continuing such aid while reliable reports implicate the police in a pattern of torture, murder, and disappearance of detainees.

II. THE MEDICOLEGAL SYSTEM IN GUATEMALA

Travelling to hospitals and morgues throughout Guatemala, we interviewed several *médicos forenses*—as physicians who practice forensic, or legal, medicine are called in Guatemala—about human rights and their country's medicolegal system. What we found was a profession demoralized after decades of military rule and years of unkept civilian promises. In interview after interview, Guatemalan forensic doctors complained about the lack of modern equipment and proper training in the forensic sciences, as well as their low salaries and often appalling working conditions. Many of them described themselves as being merely technicians who performed cursory autopsies at a breakneck pace, sent their reports to a judge, and then moved on to the next case. They never went to crime scenes to gather evidence, nor did they have regular access to witnesses' testimonies or physical evidence gathered by the police.

To understand how Guatemala's medicolegal system functions, as well as the important role it could play investigating violations of human rights, it is first necessary to take a brief look at the history and development of forensic medicine since it emerged over 700 years ago.

A. Background

Forensic medicine is the application of medicine to the resolution of legal issues. "Forensic" is a term derived from the latin word *forensus*, which means "of the forum." In ancient Rome, the forum was the site of public debate, but also served as the court where legal disputes were resolved. The first book published on forensic medicine dates back to thirteenth-century China. Entitled *Hsi Yuan Lu*, it was a handbook that Chinese physicians consulted when examining corpses in criminal cases. It told how to ascertain from a body's wounds whether a murder weapon was blunt or sharp edged.[21] It stressed the need for careful examination of the scene of the crime. And it explained how to distinguish between the cause and the manner of death.

---

[21] See Jurgen Thorwald, *The Century of the Detective* (New York: Harcourt, Brace & World, Inc., 1965), pp. 122-126.

There was nothing in Europe during the Middle Ages that remotely corresponded to this Chinese textbook. Not until 1532 did a document appear which required the participation of physicians in legal cases. It was the *Constitutio Criminalis Carolina,* also known as *The Criminal Jurisdiction of Emperor Charles V and the Holy Roman Empire,* issued by Charles V in 1532.[22] Unlike the Chinese book, this code made no mention of the need to perform autopsies where the cause of death was uncertain, although it did require the opinion of physicians when questions arose about the type of weapon used to produce certain wounds.

Three centuries later, in 1808, Napoleon issued the *Code d'instruction criminelle.* It ended the secret, inquisitorial juridical practices of preceding centuries and sought to provide a medical basis for the judgment of crimes and misdemeanors of all kinds, from murder to rape, from bodily injury to simulated illness. Most importantly, it made the forensic doctor a permanent feature of the court system.

A wholly different medicolegal system developed in Great Britain. In Europe, death investigations were handled by the judge, police, official physicians, and occasionally by specialists in forensic medicine. But in England the central figure in such cases was the coroner (from the French, *corounne,* for crown), whose office stemmed from an age–old tradition. As supervisor of the Crown's pleas, the coroner represented the king in legal matters. Among the coroner's duties was assessing and collecting taxes, including a death tax. Coroners were among the first to arrive on the scene when someone died, and took charge of investigating the circumstances surrounding suspicious deaths.

Medical expertise was not required of the coroner, who was elected and usually a friend of someone in power. Thus coroners usually got their information from questioning witnesses rather than examining corpses. Eventually, coroners began calling in university pathologists to investigate unclear cases. But even then, there was no guarantee that they possessed the special skills and expertise to diagnose crimes of violence. Trained to analyze natural causes of death, they could scarcely recognize the abnormalities that spelled violent death.

---

[22] The code also specified that one of the functions of the court physician was to determine if a defendant was strong enough to withstand torture. This requirement was dropped three decades later when Napoleon outlawed torture as a part of the legal process.

The coroner system in England was, at best, haphazard and, at worst, corrupt. But nowhere was it more slipshod and hopelessly defective than in the United States. Almost anyone, from the saloon proprietor to the undertaker, could be elected coroner. Occasionally, coroners ordered autopsies in suspicious and violent deaths, but this was the exception rather than the rule. And since few pathologists were available, they turned to general practitioners whose findings were often erroneous.

By the early 1900s, several counties and states had abandoned the coroner system for a more scientific approach: the medical examiner system. Elected coroners were replaced by physicians who had been trained in Europe in both forensic science and pathology. They became known as medical examiners. Medical examiners were usually appointed by the mayor or governor for an indefinite term unless removed from office for cause.[23]

Today medical examiners and their associates are required to be forensic pathologists certified by the American Board of Pathology following a written examination. They investigate all deaths related to trauma or that occur under suspicious circumstances or where the cause of death cannot be certified by a physician as being due to natural causes. Also, medical examiners or their death investigators frequently go to the scene to take custody of the body.

By the middle of the 20th century, forensic medicine had become a worldwide scientific discipline. Its tremendous growth was due partly to society's growing reliance on science and technology to solve problems and partly to its belief that physical and scientific evidence was more reliable than other forms, such as eye-witness accounts. Physical evidence, as one criminologist put it over thirty years ago, "is evidence that does not forget. It is not absent because human witnesses are. It is factual evidence. Physical evidence cannot be wrong; it cannot perjure itself; it cannot be wholly absent. Only its interpretation can err. Only human failure to find it, study and understand it, can diminish its value."[24]

---

[23] See News from Americas Watch, Physicians for Human Rights, and the Committee of Scientific Freedom and Responsibility of the American Association for the Advancement of Science, "The Search for Brazil's Disappeared: The Mass Grave at Dom Bosco Cemetery," (New York: March 13, 1991), pp. 14–15.

[24] See D. Kirk, Crime Investigation (New York: Interscience, 1953).

From its very beginnings forensic medicine had learned to fight and transform itself. There had been its struggle to persuade "mother" medicine of the importance of building bridges to the "lower" pursuits of jurisprudence and criminology. For a while it found physicians reluctant to leave their private clinics to enter a "grisly trade" where the rewards were puny and the chances of having one's reputation dashed in the court room were great. By mid–century, forensic medicine found that it had to make room for experts from many different disciplines, including radiology, physical anthropology, toxicology, chemistry, and genetics, whose specialized skills and expertise held great potential for expanding the capabilities of forensic work.[25]

Few, if any, of these medical and technological advances ever made it to developing countries like Guatemala. The country's military rulers had no interest in conducting medicolegal investigations of killings as they were often the perpetrators. Now, after five years of civilian rule, Guatemala's medicolegal system still evidences a considerable backwardness. "Forensic medicine in my country," as one doctor in Guatemala City put it, "is like an embryo frozen in ice, waiting to be thawed."

B. Guatemala's Death Investigation System

Guatemalan law and the rules governing its death investigation system, as in most Latin American countries, are derived from the Napoleonic code.[26] Unlike the Anglo–American system, there are no jury trials. Instead, criminal matters are investigated by judges of the first instance, or *primera instancia*, or occasionally by magistrates who are appointed by the Supreme Court for particular investigations. Investigating judges seek both exculpatory and incriminating evidence. As such, they simultaneously perform functions which, under the Anglo–American adversarial system, are carried out by both prosecutors and defense attorneys. Once the investigation is completed, the investigating judge determines whether or not there is a case against the accused and then passes it to the sentencing judge.

Guatemala's penal procedure code provides that a judge must order

---

[25] See, for example, a special issue on the forensic sciences and human rights in *The American Journal of Forensic Medicine and Pathology*, 1984;4:301–349.

[26] See, for instance, Nerio Rojas, *Medicina Legal* (Buenos Aires: El Ateneo, 1982), pp. 11–15.

an autopsy in all violent and suspicious deaths, unless the cause of death can be determined by an external examination of the body. Other provisions specify that only court–appointed doctors can perform autopsies or medical examinations in cases of rape or questioned paternity. Another provision places the country's forensic doctors and their morgues directly under the authority of the president of the Supreme Court.[27]

Guatemala's forensic doctors receive no training in forensic pathology and many have no training in anatomic pathology. Nor does the University of San Carlos--Guatemala's only public university--offer medical students residency programs in forensic medicine. To become a forensic doctor, you simply need to be a Guatemalan citizen by birth, a medical doctor, and a member of the country's medicolegal association. From then on, you learn the profession in the autopsy room.

Forensic doctors in Guatemala work either for the courts or for the national social security institute, the *Instituto Guatemalteco de Securidad Social* (IGSS). In either case, they are under the authority of the judiciary. By comparison, forensic doctors in Brazil's state–run medicolegal institutes work for the police.[28] In Guatemala, however, forensic doctors appear to have little interaction with the police.

There are some 30 forensic doctors employed by the courts in Guatemala. Of these, seven work for the judicial morgue in the capital, and the remainder are spread across the country's 22 departments. Each department has one forensic doctor, with the exception of Escuintla and Chimaltenango which have two doctors. Usually, a forensic doctor has one assistant who has no university education, let alone training in medicine.

A smaller number of forensic doctors work for Guatemala's social security service, IGSS. About 30 percent of Guatemala's population are members of IGSS, which operates its own hospitals and benefits programs. IGSS forensic doctors only conduct postmortems on deceased members, which represents one out of seven autopsies performed in the country each year. Like their counterparts in the judicial morgue, they handle all deaths resulting from violence, suicide, or occupational or traffic accidents.

---

[27] The Guatemalan military has its own morgues and forensic doctors who perform postmortems on soldiers killed while on duty.

[28] See *News From Americas Watch*, "The Search for Brazil's Disappeared."

Many Guatemalan doctors scorn "morgue work." The pay, at least in comparison to private practice, is very low, and the working conditions are archaic. As a result, many doctors who choose to work for the courts, especially in rural areas, do so to supplement their earnings from private practice or hospital positions. In one case, for instance, we learned that a forensic assistant routinely performed autopsies without the presence of the forensic doctor, who, nonetheless, signed the postmortem reports.

In December, our delegation met with Francisco Horaldo Juárez Ordóñez, a 19-year veteran of the firemen's corps of Guatemala City and its public relations officer, and Rony Iván Véliz, a fireman and newspaper reporter. They described the role the firemen and police play in death investigations.

In Guatemala, firemen are usually the first authorities to be notified when a dead body has been found. The firemen examine and photograph the body *in situ* and then call the central firestation. Next, the station's dispatcher informs the police who, in turn, notify a judge or justice of the peace. According to Juárez, the police almost always arrive at the scene before the judge. And, he added, some judges often arrive very late.

At the scene, the police gather evidence and, if witnesses are present, take testimonies. In 1987, then-Minister of the Interior Juan José Rodil Peralta told a delegation of American lawyers that most Guatemalan police officers lack even rudimentary education and are, therefore, not the best candidates for instruction in such technical matters as probable cause or forensics. According to the Minister, there are in the entire country only fifty moderately well-trained police investigators. These investigators have the equivalent of a high school education and are responsible for investigating some 2,000 homicides per year.[29]

Once the police complete their investigation, the judge orders the body transported to the judicial morgue or, if the deceased is an IGSS member, to one of the institute's morgues. The firemen performed this function until March 1990, when Supreme Court Chief Justice Edmundo Vásquez Martínez ordered that in the future the police should use their own vehicles to transport bodies. According to Juárez, the chief of police told him that the new policy was being

---

[29] See Minnesota Lawyers International Human Rights Committee, *Expectations Denied: Habeas Corpus and the Search for Guatemala's Disappeared*, (Minneapolis: January 1988), p. 43.

instituted because firemen were stealing jewelry and coins from the corpses.

Unlike forensic investigators in the United States and elsewhere, Guatemalan forensic doctors do not go to the scene to take custody of the body.[30]   Thus, they lose the opportunity to gather physical evidence, such as blood samples, hair, or fibers lying on or near the body, which untrained investigators may easily overlook.[31]   They may also lose what is referred to as contextual evidence.   This evidence includes such things as the body position and condition, including its warmth or coolness, lividity, and rigidity, as well as the body's relationship to other objects at the scene.

"In a sense, we work blindfolded," a forensic doctor in Guatemala City told us. "We receive a body at the morgue. The judge gives us a one–line report, something like 'body found on such and such a street with gunshot wound.' Now this guy could have shot himself by accident or he could have committed suicide.   Or maybe he was murdered.   But to determine which one we need more information. So we ask the police for their report on evidence they've collected at the scene.   But that gets us nowhere, because they never send it. What we need is to go to the scene ourselves, to see the body, and collect our own evidence."

In Guatemala, as in most Latin American countries, forensic doctors are only required to determine the *cause* of death, not the *manner* of death, i.e. homicide, accident, suicide, or natural causes. That determination is left to the judge, who usually has no training in medicine, let alone forensic pathology.   Thus there exists a great possibility that the manner of death may be misdiagnosed.

---

[30] Under the medical examiner system, death investigators are often sent to the scene in place of the medical examiner.   These investigators are specially trained in the handling of bodies, scene photography, and the gathering of evidence which will be useful to the forensic pathologists.

[31] The model autopsy protocol contained in the *U.N Manual on the Effective Prevention and Investigation of Extra–legal, Arbitrary and Summary Executions*, prepared by the U.N. Committee on Crime Prevention and Control in conjunction with the American Association for the Advancement of Science (AAAS) and the Minnesota Lawyers International Human Rights Committee, recommends that "medical investigators must have the right of access to the scene where the body is found. The medical personnel must be notified immediately to assure that no alteration of the body has occurred." (See Appendix C.)

An autopsy may reveal that the cause of death of a man fished from a river is asphyxiation due to his lungs' filling with enough water to halt breathing. If, however, the cause also is found to have involved a blow to the head with a crowbar, after which the unconscious victim was weighted and stuffed into a burlap bag, the investigation takes on an added air of urgency, as the manner of death obviously is homicide.

For various reasons, especially the lack of funds, Guatemalan forensic doctors are unable to perform several standard autopsy procedures. For one thing, they do not routinely photograph all bodies at autopsy.[32] Nor do they have regular access to X-ray equipment or fluoroscopes, which, among other things, aid in locating bullets and other projectiles in the body.

One of the most disquieting moments during our visit came as we toured Guatemala City's judicial morgue. Our hosts were two forensic doctors who worked at the morgue. They apologized profusely for the conditions in the facility's autopsy room, but wanted us to see first-hand the conditions under which they worked. Their autopsy instruments were more like the tools found in butcher shops and garden sheds than those used by forensic doctors. The room itself, with its four autopsy tables, was cramped and lacked proper ventilation. There were no refrigeration units and only one sink. The only containers available for holding specimens were old jam jars piled up in a corner gathering dust and cobwebs. What appeared to be a small, dingy closet directly adjacent to the autopsy room was actually the examining room for rape victims. One of our hosts, clearly embarrassed and ashamed by the room, asked us to try to imagine what it was like for the unfortunate women who were brought there, often at night, for examinations.

After leaving the autopsy room, we climbed a staircase to a one-room dormitory on the floor above. The dormitory was occupied by guards who work day and night shifts. Fortunately, a balcony adjacent to the room provided them relief in summer from the stench below. The guards said they had to buy their own cots and bedding and small gas stoves for cooking. It would be easy to dismiss such

---

[32] The U.N. model autopsy protocol maintains that "adequate photographs are crucial for thorough documentation of autopsy findings." Of particular importance, it states, are photographs that "confirm the presence of all demonstrable signs of injury or disease commented upon in the autopsy report." Such documentation, it adds, is particularly important in an autopsy performed in a controversial death.

conditions as simply the manifestations of underdevelopment. But that would be only part of the story.

We left the morgue and walked twenty yards to a large, one–story building. Our hosts led us inside and into a room the size of a basketball court. Long fluorescent bulbs hung from the ceiling. In the center of the room were twelve stainless steel autopsy tables. Next to each table, against the wall, was a sink and a work station, also made of stainless steel. Along a wall a few yards from the autopsy room stretched a bank of refrigerators that would have been the envy of any small–town coroner in England or the United States. One of our hosts opened a refrigerator door and pointed to several rusty hinges. The refrigeration units, like everything else in the morgue, he said, had never been used.

Built in 1988, this building was to have replaced the older morgue next door, only the forensic doctors never received the authorization to move in. Instead, several judges were assigned to the building's administrative offices and have remained there ever since. Morgue facilities in rural Guatemala are even worse than those in the capital. The judicial morgue in Santa Cruz del Quiché, the capital for the Department of Quiché, for instance, is located in the parking garage of the National Hospital. It consists of one room, an autopsy table, and a small sink with no running water. There is often no electricity for the single light bulb. Although the hospital has an X–ray machine, the morgue never uses it because the cost of film is prohibitive.

These days, the morgue's forensic doctor, Ana Lisette García de Crocker, and her assistant, Flavio A. Montúfar Dardón, manage to "get by" with the space provided. However, in the early 1980s, as troops made bloody sweeps through the highlands and death squads prowled the city's streets, the floor of the small, one–room morgue was often covered with bodies. According to Montúfar, the morgue often received between eight and fifteen bodies a day. One day the number rose to fifty–one. Many of the bodies from that period showed signs of torture. In recent years, the number of bodies received by the morgue has diminished considerably, averaging in 1990 between twelve and fifteen bodies a month.

In 1987, the then–director of Guatemala City's judicial morgue, Dr. Abel Girón, told a delegation from the Minnesota Lawyers International Human Rights Committee that during the presidency of General Romeo Lucas García (1978 – 1982), many corpses were discovered with marks of torture, such as broken fingers and missing fingernails.[33]   Dr. Girón said that the government was so secure in its power that it was glad to have forensic doctors reveal the signs of torture as a deterrent to would-be subversives.   He also said that he rarely saw such obvious torture marks any more.

The forensic doctors we spoke with in Guatemala City confirmed Dr. Girón's observations, although several of them said they still saw bodies bearing signs of torture.   They also noted there had been a rise in violent deaths in recent years.   For instance, the number of autopsied bodies killed by firearms and other deadly weapons such as machetes declined from 48% in 1981 to an average of about 21% in 1987.[34]   By 1989, however, the number had risen to 42%.[35]   In addition, in the first six months of 1989 the number of firearm-related deaths (332) was very high.   Of these, 51% (170) were attributed to single gunshot wounds to the head.   Such wounds suggest that many of these deaths were execution-style killings.

Because the field of forensic medicine rests on the concept of a legitimate government authority, forensic doctors face a distressful and dangerous situation when the state itself subverts the system of justice. Doctors who produce autopsy findings that implicate government authorities or their agents may pay with their jobs or even their lives. In Guatemala, it appears that forensic doctors have, at least in recent years, been free of pressure from their superiors or the police to falsify autopsy findings.   As one forensic doctor in Guatemala City put it: "When it comes to threats, they don't waste their time on us.   We're not that important.   The killers are immune: they'll never be

---

[33] See Minnesota Lawyers, *Expectations Denied*, p. 41.

[34] *Ibid.*

[35] The total deaths by year in which autopsies were performed by the judicial morgue in Guatemala City are as follows:

1981	2,745
1982	2,312
1983	2,119
1984	1,904
1985	1,905
1986	2,246
1987	953 (January through May only)
1988	N/A
1989	2,590

convicted, let alone prosecuted, especially on the basis of an autopsy finding. Not here."

Such sentiments notwithstanding, another doctor told us that after he attended a seminar on human rights someone began watching his house. In addition, a fireman who helped exhume several unmarked graves in the highlands in 1990 reportedly received a series of threatening telephone calls.[36] The calls stopped, however, after the firemen's association ran a notice protesting the death threats in several newspapers.

---

[36] Interview with Francisco Juárez Ordóñez and Rony Iván Véliz, in Guatemala City, December 11, 1990.

III. DISAPPEARANCES, TORTURE AND EXTRAJUDICIAL KILLINGS

The Guatemalan military is credited with having introduced the use of "disappearances" as a repressive tool to the Americas in the late 1960s, a technique practiced twenty years earlier by the Nazis as a means of eliminating opposition without creating martyrs.[37] Since the 1960s, when the Guatemalan army first faced a challenge from leftist insurgents, it has made tens of thousands of people -- trade unionists, leftist political activists, students, teachers, peasant and human rights activists, and many people suspected only of having contacts with or sympathizing with guerrillas -- "disappear." Most of the disappeared are presumed to have been killed after a period of torture and interrogation. Many more have simply been killed. Although the insurgents were decimated in the military campaigns of the early 1980s, the Guatemalan army's "dirty war" grinds on. Today a 42,000-man army faces a rebel force of little more than 1,000.

Very few victims have survived torture or disappearance in Guatemala. Often the bodies of the disappeared, bearing signs of torture or mutilation, are found dumped in ravines or by the sides of roads. The rare testimony from a survivor indicates that both the police and military operate clandestine detention centers where they interrogate their victims under torture, including beatings, rape, burning with cigarettes, application of electric shocks, suffocation with a rubber hood, burning with acid, and forced inhalation of toxins. Bodies are sometimes found with parts -- eyes, ears, tongues, hands -- removed.

During the military regimes of the late 1970s and early 1980s, and particularly during the presidency of General Romeo Lucas García, repression was known to be highly centralized; those targeted for torture, disappearance, or assassination were selected by the president and senior ministers in meetings held in an annex to the National Palace in Guatemala City.[38] Few people believe the civilian leadership in either the Cerezo or Serrano administrations personally direct the terror. But it is clear that army intelligence (G-2) is responsible for at least some of the torture, disappearances, and

---

[37] Amnesty International USA, 'Disappearances': A Workbook, (New York: 1981), pp. 1-2.

[38] Amnesty International, Guatemala: A Government Program of Political Murder, (London: 1981).

killings.[39]   The agency's historic role in tracking and eliminating enemies of the army has led it to be called "the unelected government of Guatemala."[40]

In recent years, survivors have testified that torture takes place in various military barracks and police precincts, including the third floor of the National Police headquarters in Guatemala City (see below). A former G-2 technician described to Americas Watch in a March 21, 1991 interview several clandestine detention centers in Guatemala City where the military secretly tortures detainees.   According to the technician, who wishes to remain anonymous for fear of reprisals, the G-2 operated a torture center in the laundry room of the old Military Politechnical Academy in Guatemala City, until the Human Rights Ombudsman visited the location.   Having been warned of the functionary's impending visit, the G-2 cleared out the center's premises and moved it to a renovated building in Zone 17 near the Mariscal Zavala military barracks. (The G-2 headquarters is located inside the National Palace.) The Mobile Military Police headquarters in Zone 6 also has clandestine torture cells, the technician said.

Another low-ranking former G-2 employee interviewed in 1988 described being assigned to compile lists of names of individuals in the Defense Ministry inside the National Palace based on newspaper clippings and information from National Police computer files. He stated that he learned from a colleague that he was compiling army hit lists.[41]

In addition to the police and military, Guatemala's civil patrols are increasingly agents of repression and assassination. The civil patrols were organized by the military in the early 1980s to extend and consolidate its control over the farflung villages of Guatemala's highland provinces, whose population had, in large part, been won over by the guerrillas in the late 1970s.   Under the military governments of General Efraín Ríos Montt (March 1982 – August 1983) and General Humberto Mejía Víctores (August 1983 – January

---

[39] During the Cerezo administration, the G-2 was renamed "D-2". Nonetheless, it is more commonly referred to by its previous name.

[40] Allan Nairn and Jean-Marie Simon, "The Bureaucracy of Death," *The New Republic*, June 30, 1986, p. 13.

[41] See Americas Watch, *Closing the Space*, p. 17, and International Human Rights Law Group, *Maximizing Deniability: The Justice System and Human Rights in Guatemala*, (Washington, D.C.: July 1989), pp. 83 – 84.

1986), all highland males between the ages of 15 and 60 were compelled to serve in the civil patrols, in shifts of 12 to 24 hours every week or two depending on the number of men in the community. However, Guatemala's new Constitution, which came into force in January 1986, prohibited compulsory patrolling, a provision which has been blatantly and widely disregarded by the military and local patrol chiefs. Moreover, a strong element of discrimination has been applied, as invariably it is the Indian men who are forced to patrol, while the mixed-race *ladinos* are almost always exempted.

The patrollers are required to guard entrances to villages, stop and question visitors, and report to local army commanders on "subversive" activities of their neighbors. Sometimes the army forces patrollers to perform menial labor, such as collecting firewood or guarding machinery. In addition, the army delegates to the patrols its most dangerous work, such as walking point on mountain sweeps in search of guerrilla columns. The patrollers -- some of whom carry World War II-vintage M-1 rifles, others machetes or sticks -- are armed sufficiently to menace civilians but not adequately to defend themselves from guerrillas. On February 16, 1991, for example, guerrillas ambushed and killed ten patrollers as they followed army instructions to take down a sheet with guerrilla slogans draped over a bridge in Playa Grande, El Quiché. Yet while individual patrollers may be the army's cannon fodder, the patrol chiefs have become the army's local enforcers: little dictators endowed with the power of life and death. Many of the cases investigated by our delegation were murders carried out or ordered by local patrol chiefs (see especially Chapter VII).

This report presents six examples of medicolegal investigations into recent human rights abuses, including the assassinations of human rights activists, the torture and murder of street children, the massacre of Tzutujil Indians at Santiago Atitlán, and the murder of villagers by a local patrol chief in 1984. The cases are diverse both geographically and in terms of the alleged perpetrators -- who include the army, civil patrollers, and the police -- and represent differing degrees of effort on the part of the authorities. Yet almost all have led to the same result: impunity.

A. Sebastián Velásquez Mejía, Chunimá

Sebastián Velásquez Mejía, 39, was the most outspoken human rights activist in the hamlet of Chunimá, which lies in the hills several kilometers down a dirt road from the Pan American Highway in the department of El Quiché. Velásquez was the local representative for both the Council of Ethnic Communities "We Are All Equal" (CERJ) and the Mutual Support Group (GAM) and the spokesperson for those in the village who resisted incorporation into the civil patrols.

Since May 1988, when Chunimá men formally resigned from the civil patrols, Velásquez had frequently been threatened and harassed by soldiers. After a group of villagers reformed a civil patrol in Chunimá, the patrol chiefs began to threaten Velásquez as well. One of them, in the course of a village meeting in May 1989, vowed he'd cut off Velásquez's head with a machete, according to a complaint filed by villagers with the Human Rights Ombudsman. In February 1990, after Chunimá residents had submitted half a dozen complaints to the Ombudsman and other authorities about these threats, the commander of Military Base #20 in Santa Cruz del Quiché sent his own complaint to the Human Rights Ombudsman, charging that villagers from Chunimá, first among them Velásquez, "constantly pester" the civil patrols in Chunimá by throwing rocks at their guardposts and sending "unfounded" complaints to the Human Rights Ombudsman.[42] Clearly the army and patrol chiefs viewed Velásquez as a major troublemaker.

On October 6, 1990, Velásquez was kidnapped while waiting for a bus to Guatemala City to buy medicine for his children. Our delegation interviewed three witnesses to his abduction as well as the judge investigating the case. According to their account, shortly before Velásquez arrived at the bus stop at kilometer 110 of the Pan American Highway, a blue Toyota pickup truck with smoked glass windows pulled up on the opposite side of the highway. One of the five men in civilian clothes riding in the truck got out and walked over to the local civil patrol chief, Manuel Perebal Ajtzalam III, who was standing in front of a store, and talked with him for several minutes. The chief, Perebal Ajtzalam III, indicated to the man the place where Velásquez was standing. The plainclothesman then

---

[42] The CERJ and GAM have maintained voluminous files of complaints from Chunimá residents to various government agencies regarding the frequent threats and harassment by the army and civil patrols which Velásquez and other residents suffered.

returned to the truck, after which two of the men grabbed Velásquez, shoved him in the back of the truck, and sat on top of him as the pickup took off in the direction of Guatemala City. The witnesses recognized the pickup as the same one the army uses each month to make payments to soldiers at the military stockade at Chupol.

At 9:45 a.m. on October 8, a body with Velásquez's identification card was found on Avenida del Ferrocarril, between 2nd and 3rd street in Guatemala City's Zone 9. An autopsy was performed in Guatemala City's Judicial Morgue at 11:35 a.m. The autopsy report described the cause of death as "fourth degree contusion" to the thorax and abdomen. The autopsy also described bruises on the cranium, liver, and lungs, pulmonary edema, visceral congestion, and "fatty change in the liver." On October 10, the body was placed in a plastic body bag and buried in Guatemala City's La Verbena Cemetery.

Although the CERJ had filed *habeas corpus* petitions within minutes of the kidnapping, and the GAM within days, neither were informed of the discovery and burial of the body. It was not until October 18 that family members received the news. However, the description of the body and clothing provided to relatives by the police Identification Bureau (*Gabinete de Identificación*), left the family doubtful as to whether the body buried in La Verbena Cemetery really was Velásquez. Velásquez's common-law wife requested exhumation of the body to identify it. The district court denied the request on the grounds that Velásquez's companion, who is the mother of his five children, did not have standing as the two were not legally married. Nor could the couple's minor children make the request.

In response to a press communiqué by the GAM, the National Police issued a statement published in the Guatemalan press on November 17 claiming that Velásquez had never been kidnapped, but had come to the capital of his own volition, where he died of alcohol intoxication.[43] This statement added urgency to the desire on the part of Velásquez's friends and colleagues in the human rights movement to conduct an exhumation, not only to identify the body, but also to prove how Velásquez died.

On December 3, with the assistance of the Archbishop of Guatemala's Human Rights Office, another of Velásquez's relatives

---

[43] "GAM denuncia secuestro y asesinato de campesino," *Siglo Veintiuno*, November 16, 1990; "Policía refuta al GAM," *Siglo Veintiuno*, November 17, 1990; and "Cerezo's Violent Legacy," *Central America Report*, Vol. XVII No. 46, November 30, 1990, p. 1.

presented an exhumation request. The petition asked that the members of our delegation be present as experts. This time, the request was granted.

The afternoon before the exhumation, Snow and Kirschner spent several hours with Velásquez's family recording physical characteristics which might assist in identification of the corpse and probing his history of alcohol use. The court–ordered exhumation took place on December 12. Although the body was in a state of decomposition, Velásquez's widow recognized it as her husband. In addition, dental cavities, facial features, and a scar on the back of the right arm fit the description relatives had provided. Unfortunately, the judge would not permit the body to be taken to a morgue so that a second autopsy could be performed, which might have lent more useful information to determine how Velásquez died. The judge denied the request on the grounds that the exhumation was only ordered for identification purposes. As a result, Velásquez's family went through the trauma of watching the unearthing of their loved one in a decomposed state while gaining only a portion of the medical information that could have been learned. Nonetheless, the controversial police assertion that Velásquez died from drinking was denied by Dr. Alonso René Portillo, who stated that toxicological analysis of Velásquez's blood performed in October did not reveal signs of alcoholic intoxication.

Although he was not permitted to perform a second autopsy, Dr. Kirschner's external examination of the body led him to question the conclusions in the autopsy report, as he did not find signs of the contusions described, which he said should have been detectable even after two months' decomposition. In addition, during the removal of the body from the grave, the previously removed crown of the skull came loose and it became apparent that the brain had never been removed from the head. Yet the autopsy stated that the brain weighed 1,350 grams, a conclusion which could not have been reached without the organ's removal. Absent an internal examination of the body, Dr. Kirschner could not confirm the cause of Velásquez's death. He noted that asphyxiation was a possibility, given the absence of external injuries and the fact that Velásquez had been kidnapped two days before his body was found.

Following the exhumation, the case was transferred to the Second District Court in Santa Cruz del Quiché, under whose jurisdiction the kidnapping occurred. The judge proceeded to interview the three men who saw Velásquez's kidnapping, and on January 21, issued an arrest warrant for Manuel Perebal Ajtzalam III, the civil patrol chief of Chunimá said to have fingered Velásquez to the kidnappers.

The police, however, did not make any attempt to arrest Perebal Ajtzalam III. And on February 17, 1991, Perebal Ajtzalam III, another Chunimá patrol chief, and four other men shot two of the witnesses to the Velásquez kidnapping along with their father as they were walking towards Chupol to shop at the market. Manuel Perebal Morales, who testified about Velásquez's kidnapping to our delegation, and subsequently to the judge, died in the attack, as did his father, Juan Perebal Xirúm. His half–brother, Diego Perebal León, who also testified to our delegation and the court, was gravely wounded with bullet wounds in the arm and abdomen, leaving one leg paralyzed. All three were members of the CERJ.

The next day, a justice of the peace in Chichicastenango issued a new arrest warrant for Perebal Ajtzalam III, along with Manuel León Lares, the other patrol chief identified by the survivor as one of the gunmen. This judicial order too, was ignored. The Second District Court judge, clearly distressed by the police flaunting of judicial authority, told Americas Watch that the Chunimá patrollers have "tremendous impunity." He complained that his efforts to press the newly appointed Interior Minister, Ricardo Méndez Ruiz, nominally in charge of the police, to carry out the arrests, had been frustrated when the minister did not return the judge's phone calls.[44] So confident was Perebal Ajtzalam III that he would never be brought to justice, the judge said, that he was overheard boasting to a group of peasants: "I wipe my ass with arrest warrants."

In a May 3 letter to Senator Alan Cranston, who had written to him about the case, President Serrano stated "In fact today I can report that all suspects are in Police custody." President Serrano apparently based this mistaken assertion on the fact that he had personally ordered the arrests to be carried out. Yet when the police attempted to arrest the patrollers in Chunimá on April 26, a hostile crowd of patrollers blocked their effort.[45] During a meeting with leaders of the CERJ and CERJ members from Chunimá on June 4, 1991, Serrano

---

[44] In early May 1991, President Serrano appointed a new Interior Minister, former adjunct human rights ombudsman Fernando Hurtado Prem.

[45] See Lee Hockstader, "Guatemalan Village Becomes Arena for Human Rights Struggle," *The Washington Post*, May 24, 1991; and Shirley Christian, "Guatemala Defense Patrol: Force in its Own Right," *The New York Times*, June 2, 1991.

again contended that the patrollers had been arrested, according to CERJ leader Amílcar Méndez. When the CERJ members insisted they were still at large, Serrano asked a subordinate to bring him a National Police list of recent arrests. There he found the names of the patrollers -- Manuel Perebal Ajtzalam III and Manuel León Lares -- with the word "pending" next to them, Méndez said. The president then vowed to have the men arrested promptly.

The police made a second effort to arrest the patrol chiefs on June 13, but again were rebuffed. Their second inadequate effort only served to endanger further human rights activists in Chunimá. Immediately after the police fled Chunimá, Manuel Perebal Ajtzalam III and his brother, Tomás Perebal Ajtzalam, went to the home of a GAM member whom they accused of helping the police. The men beat, kicked, and threatened the man, Tomás Velásquez Ajtzalam, and stole his machete, according to testimony from Chunimá residents taken by the CERJ. The patrollers also briefly detained and threatened a young CERJ member who guided the police into the village, Manuel Xaper Velásquez.

As of this writing, the police have still not arrested the suspects, despite the fact that they continue to live in their communities and threaten human rights activists living there. Diego Perebal León has taken refuge with the CERJ in Santa Cruz del Quiché, along with fifteen members of his family who were evacuated from Chunimá by the adjunct human rights ombudsman in March to save them from further violence at the hands of the patrollers.

B. María Mejía, Parraxtut

At 7:30 p.m. on March 17, 1990, two armed men came to the house of María Mejía and her common-law husband, Pedro Castro Tojín, claiming to be members of the Guerrilla Army of the Poor (*Ejército Guerrillero de los Pobres*). Castro Tojín shone a flashlight in the men's faces and recognized them as two local military commissioners[46] who had been threatening the family because of its membership in human rights groups and refusal to patrol. The two men, Domingo Castro Lux and Juan de León Pérez, shot Mejía and Castro Tojín as they stood at their doorstep, and then shot them again

---

[46] Military commissioners are civilians hired and armed by the military to gather intelligence and assist in recruitment.

after they fell back into the house, Castro Tojín told Americas Watch shortly after the killing. Then they ran off.[47]

Castro Tojín managed to drag himself to a neighbor's house, arriving at about 9:00 p.m. The next day, the neighbors went to the nearest town, Sacapulas, to tell the justice of the peace of the attack. At about 3:15 p.m., two justices of the peace and three National Police agents arrived at the scene. By the time they arrived, most of Mejía's face had been eaten by dogs. According to a witness interviewed by our delegation, the police found one shell from a Galil rifle under the body, which they took with them.

Mejía's body was taken to the morgue in Santa Cruz del Quiché, where a superficial examination was performed by the assistant to the forensic doctor. No autopsy was conducted and no bullets recovered from the body. The death certificate states only that Mejía died instantly of brain hemorrhage (*atrición cerebral*), as a result of a skull fractured by gunshots.

Equally inadequate was the crime scene investigation. The justice of the peace identified the body, ordered it transferred to the morgue, and ordered the police to take testimony from the neighbor who had notified the authorities of the crime, according to the judge in the Second District Court in Santa Cruz del Quiché. The justice of the peace failed to draw a map of the scene, or to look for shells, bootprints or tire tracks. No photographs were taken. No effort was made to determine where the shots that killed Mejía were fired from. If indeed the police recovered a shell under Mejía's body, as a witness told our delegation, they failed to turn over this evidence to the judge.

These initial shortcomings in the death investigation were compounded as the case proceeded. In the days following the assassination, the suspected killers threatened to kill members of three families active in human rights groups if they did not leave Parraxtut. Twenty-nine villagers took refuge in Santa Cruz del Quiché, most of them crowding into the office of the CERJ. On March 27, a caravan including the displaced villagers, CERJ President Amílcar Méndez, adjunct human rights ombudsman César Alvarez Guadamuz, the assistant ombudsman from Santa Cruz, and two National Police officers went to Parraxtut. Adjunct ombudsman Alvarez Guadamuz intended to return the villagers to their homes and instruct the local patrollers and military commissioners not to harm them. The National

---

[47] See *News From Americas Watch*, "Guatemala: Army Campaign," pp. 3 – 8.

Police agents carried arrest warrants which they intended to serve on the suspects. Yet unbeknownst to them, army officers from Nebaj had visited Parraxtut early that morning and instructed villagers, patrollers and military commissioners to gird themselves with guns, machetes, sticks, and rocks to "break" the delegation, whose members they described as communists. When Alvarez Guadamuz, Méndez and the others arrived at the village, hundreds of armed patrollers, military commissioners, and plainclothes soldiers greeted them with hostility, first threatening Méndez and then firing on him and the villagers as they fled. The mob then detained, threatened, and harassed Alvarez Guadamuz and the others for about an hour.[48] Thoroughly intimidated by the experience, the police did not arrest the suspects on that day, nor did they make any subsequent attempts to arrest them. Nonetheless, just in case they should be detained, the patrol chief of Parraxtut allegedly called a meeting on April 14 where villagers who could read and write were recruited to serve as false alibi witnesses for the suspected killers.[49] Finally on May 15, the army brought the suspects to the court, reportedly after assuring them that they would be freed for lack of evidence.

Although the judge who interviewed the survivor and sole witness, Castro Tojín, found him credible, under Guatemalan law his testimony can be disregarded by virtue of his relationship to the victim. Thus when alibi witnesses testified that the defendants had been in Guatemala City at the time of the shooting -- testimony we believe to be perjured -- the judge decided there was insufficient evidence to try them and ordered them released. This decision was upheld on appeal. The attorney general's office made only a perfunctory appeal, and did not even send a prosecutor to the hearing. Meanwhile attorneys for the CERJ were obliged to drop their appeal and cease providing the CERJ with legal assistance after receiving written death threats from a previously unheard of group which calls itself the Utatlán Indigenous Movement.[50] Although the case is technically

---

[48] Ibid., pp. 5-6.

[49] Ibid., p. 7.

[50] Subsequently, flyers were distributed in Santa Cruz del Quiché signed by the same group calling on the indigenous population to slay members and "collaborators" of the CERJ. See News From Americas Watch, "Guatemala: Rights Abuses Escalate," p. 18.

"under investigation" again at the trial court, no further action has been taken and it is likely to remain in that state indefinitely.

Clearly the absence of any medical or scientific evidence in this case helped steer it into this dead end. The provision of the Criminal Procedure Code (Article 655) which allows judges to discard the testimony of relatives is also to blame. By assuming that relatives are so interested as to be incapable of providing reliable testimony, this rule mounts a needless and highly destructive obstacle to ascertaining the truth and thus holding accountable the perpetrators of crimes.[51] A judge reviewing the case for our delegation noted that the presiding judge had not cross-examined the defendants or the alibi witnesses to test their credibility, which he described as typical. In the absence of forensic evidence and cross-examination of witnesses, anyone who denies committing a crime usually gets off, the judge remarked.

C. Myrna Elizabeth Mack Chang

Myrna Mack, 40, was a British-educated anthropologist and one of the founders of Guatemala's preeminent social science research institute, the Association for the Advancement of the Social Sciences in Guatemala (AVANCSO). She conducted research on the situation of those Guatemalans displaced by the counterinsurgency campaigns of the late 1970s and early 1980s.

On September 11, 1990, Mack was stabbed to death upon leaving her office in Guatemala City. The political sensitivity of her work, which placed her directly at odds with the army over a matter it considered of vital importance; the fact that she had been under surveillance at her home and office for weeks before her death; and the more than 25 stab wounds inflicted -- unusual in cases of robbery -- quickly led to suspicions that the military was behind her murder. Tragically, the complete failure of the authorities to investigate adequately her death is likely to preclude identification and criminal prosecution of her assassins.

Our delegation interviewed Mack's sister, the doctor who performed the autopsy, a senior police investigations officer, the judge in charge of the case at the time, officials in the Attorney General's office, the Human Rights Ombudsman, and others with knowledge about the

---

[51] Another rule, Article 654, provides similar obstacles to the prosecution of criminal acts. This rule requires a judge, among other things, to disregard absolutely testimony from a witness who holds "grave and manifest enmity toward the person against whom he/she is declaring."

case. We also examined court documents which had been provided to the Mack family. In addition, Dr. Kirschner analyzed forensic evidence including crime scene and autopsy photographs, the autopsy report, and the clothing Mack wore at the time of her death. His findings are included as an appendix to this report and are summarized below. The report has been provided to a Guatemalan forensic doctor contracted by Mack's family to prepare an independent report on the evidence for the criminal court investigating the case.

Myrna Mack's Work on the Displaced

Ever since the military's counterinsurgency campaigns in the highland provinces of Alta Verapaz, Huehuetenango, El Quiché, and Chimaltenango, which by the army's own estimate destroyed 440 villages, hundreds of thousands of the survivors either have been displaced from their communities or fled the country. Indeed, at the height of the repression, about 20 percent of the population was internally displaced.[52] Tens of thousands went into hiding in remote pockets of the highlands' mountainous terrain or the northern jungle lowlands. In 1983, the army began resettling the displaced in strategic hamlets euphemistically called "model villages," whose residents enjoy virtually no freedom of movement and who live under constant surveillance by the army and civil patrols. In late 1987, the Army launched an offensive designed, in large part, to relocate thousands of civilians still hiding in the mountains. Control of this population, in the eyes of the army, is fundamental to its continued domination of areas whose population supported the guerrillas in the late 1970s and early 1980s.

Although foreign researchers have been able to study conditions in some conflictive areas for several years, fear of assassination has forced most Guatemalan researchers to remain within the geographical confines of their offices in the capital. Mack was the first Guatemalan social scientist in years to conduct field research in the highlands. Mack's last written study, published jointly by AVANCSO and Georgetown University's Hemispheric Migration Project, carefully documented the military chokehold over the displaced. The report called for demilitarization of the process of return and reintegration of

---

[52] Asociación Para el Avance de las Ciencias Sociales en Guatemala (AVANCSO), "The Context of Myrna Mack's Violent Death," Guatemala City, November 1990, p. 1.

40

the displaced, and the establishment of civilian control over the vast highland areas currently under *de facto* military rule.[53]

Although the displaced have long suffered in anonymity, their plight has been thrust into the forefront of public debate in Guatemala after Mack's assassination. A movement to allow those thousands hiding from the army to emerge from clandestiness and enjoy the rights of civilians living under a democracy is gathering momentum. If indeed Mack's assassination was an effort by the army to silence her political views, it has backfired.

Surveillance of Mack's Home and Office

On September 1, ten days before her murder, Mack's family was alerted to the fact that their house had been under surveillance by three men in civilian clothes between August 27–31. On one occasion, two of the men were seen on a motorcycle following Mack's sister, who looks like her. The motorcycle violated several traffic regulations as it pursued her car.[54] Physical descriptions of the men on the motorcycle have been provided to the judge investigating the case and sketches, based on these descriptions, have been drawn.

Between September 3–10, the AVANCSO office came under surveillance, a fact which Mack's colleagues learned only after her death. A gray van with smoked glass windows was seen outside the office every day that week. And a hot dog vendor appeared on the street, situated strategically to observe the comings and goings of the AVANCSO staff. The vendor had not been noticed there before or since, and did not appear to have the required license plates. Two men in civilian clothes were also seen hanging around near the office entrance after 4:30 p.m. on September 11.[55] Mack was stabbed to death at approximately 6:45 or 7:00 p.m. that evening, just after leaving the office.

---

[53] AVANCSO, *Assistance and Control: Policies Toward Internally Displaced Populations in Guatemala*, (Washington, D.C.: Center for Immigration Policy and Refugee Assistance, Georgetown University, 1990), p. 49.

[54] AVANCSO, "The Context," p. 5.

[55] Ibid.

The Death Investigation

Of all the cases our delegation reviewed, this was the one most thoroughly investigated by Guatemalan authorities. The fact that this represents a sort of best-case scenario for an investigation into a human rights case in Guatemala is a powerful indictment of the system. Dr. Kirschner's report on the crime scene investigation (see Appendix A) concludes "there was a total failure to process the crime scene in an appropriate manner, and to retain evidence necessary for the evaluation of this case." Although the National Police sent one of its mobile crime labs, donated by the United States, to the scene, it failed to provide any useful information. The mobile lab was commanded by José Estuardo Méndez Vásquez, the chief of the National Police Identification Bureau (*Gabinete de Identificación*). The National Police Director, Colonel Julio Caballeros Seigne, was also present at the scene, yet failed to ensure that evidence was gathered and preserved.

Photographs of the body and surrounding area taken by the voluntary firemen who came first to the scene and subsequent shots taken by the police identification bureau make clear that Mack struggled hard with her assailant (or assailants); the walls of the nearest building and the sidewalk are spattered with blood. Bloody footprints -- possibly those of the killers -- surround the corpse. The police have given different explanations of the footprints, telling a relative they undoubtedly were the footprints of curious onlookers but telling a member of our delegation they were the footprints of the firemen. If any analysis of the footprints was conducted by the police, the results were not submitted to the judge. Dr. Kirschner's analysis of the footprints, based on enlargements of the photographs, concludes that they belonged to some kind of boot and were probably present prior to the scene being disturbed by the firemen and the police. Laboratory analysis of the prints could have provided evidence as to the number of different prints and their size, style, and possibly even manufacture. However, this evidence is now lost forever.

One of the police photographs shows Mack's left hand grasping a length of clear or white plastic material (see photograph). The plastic is twisted and is consistent with a ligature that might have been placed around her neck. Mack's arms and right hand bear several "defense" wounds, which give testimony to the violence of the struggle; her left hand, which grasped the plastic, has no such wounds. This evidence suggests that Mack's assailant(s) may have intended to kidnap her, but ended up killing her when she fought more than they had expected.

The length of twisted plastic which appears in the photograph might have been wrapped around her neck by one assailant, while another threatened her with a knife. It is also possible that the ligature was intended to bind her hands.

The plastic found in Mack's hand was an important piece of evidence which should have been analyzed by the police, reported on, and turned over to the judge. This had not been done at the time of our meeting with the judge on December 12. On December 18, 1990, in response to an inquiry by the judge, police identification bureau chief Méndez stated that the piece of plastic "was submitted at the scene to a search for any kind of evidence with no results," and then discarded.[56] This flies in the face of proper investigative procedures, including preservation of evidence found at the crime scene.

Another explanation was provided by the police Criminal Investigations Department (*Departamento de Investigaciones Criminológicas*, DIC), in a caption to the photograph provided to the judge before our visit. The DIC caption described the twisted piece of plastic as "the piece of the plastic handle of the bag in the left hand of the deceased which was stolen..." Yet there is no testimony that Mack was carrying a plastic bag when she left her office or that such a bag was stolen. And, assuming the police at the scene found this theory plausible, they were negligent in not retaining the piece of plastic for a possible match with the rest of the "bag," which might have been taken by the assailant(s).

Dr. Kirschner's analysis of the enlarged photograph of the plastic further discounts the notion of a robbery attempt. "If this was a robbery," Kirschner states, "there would have been no reason for such a violent struggle to retain possession of a shopping bag. If the bag had been literally 'ripped off,' the handle portion remaining in Myrna's hand should have been stretched and showed frayed ends. In fact, the plastic is moderately twisted, appears too long to be a bag handle, and is thus more likely to be a ligature."

Police at the scene of the crime reportedly placed plastic bags on Mack's hands so that the forensic doctor performing the autopsy could analyze them for trace evidence associated with the struggle. Yet such analysis was never undertaken. The physician who performed the autopsy a few hours after the murder told our delegation that police officers had already removed the bags and fingerprinted Mack's hands

---

[56] Letter dated December 18, 1990 from José Estuardo Méndez Vásquez, Chief, National Police Bureau of Identification, to First District Court Judge.

before the doctor arrived, thus destroying any evidence that he might have found.

The clothing Mack was wearing at the time of her death were given to her sister without being examined by forensic laboratory personnel, thereby losing the opportunity to retrieve trace evidence from her attacker(s). Although they had subsequently been washed, the clothes were later turned over to Kirschner for analysis of the tears.

Finally, the police appear to have made no effort to establish what government agency had Mack under surveillance. And although witnesses have provided physical descriptions of the men who were watching Mack's home and office before her death, we are aware of no effort by the police to find and apprehend these men.

Serrano Government Offers Red Herring

The Serrano government's actions on this case, which occurred during the last year of the Cerezo presidency, do not inspire confidence either. A report presented to the diplomatic corps by President Serrano on March 1, 1991, suggests that Mack was attempting "urgently" to make a black market transaction to change into dollars local currency worth $9,000 and for that reason "may have been the object of persecution by criminals." The basis for this assertion is not fully explained in the report, which simply itemizes two blank checks Mack allegedly received from her parents, as well as a "transfer" (giro) of $441.

Mack's parents responded with indignation over the report's suggestions in a March 12, 1991 letter to the diplomatic corps. "We are enormously concerned that this report from the government of the Republic, which is a response to the many petitions from the international community, does not contribute to solving the case and only causes confusion, as well as making one think that a genuine interest to get to the bottom of the issue does not exist," Mack's parents wrote. The letter denied that Mack was trying to obtain $9,000, explaining that the only financial transaction she was engaged in at the time of her death was the purchase in quetzales of an airplane ticket to Canada for a student exchange program for her teenage daughter. The first "blank check" mentioned in the President's report, Mack's parents added, was in fact a check from her own account. The second check described in the report has the wrong account number. The "transfer" for $441 dollars, they add, was not a transfer, but rather a personal check to pay for her daughter's expenses in Canada.

The letter goes on to state that investigating the cashing of checks only takes thirty days (while the President's report came nearly six months after the murder), and notes that the checks mentioned were never cashed. Mack's parents deny that she needed to change –– or had ever changed –– money on the black market; or that she had any urgent need for money, as all the expenses for her daughter's exchange program had been covered.

As this report was going to print, Attorney General Acisclo Valladares announced that the court had identified a suspect, Noel de Jesús Beteta Alvarez, in the murder of Myrna Mack. One press account referred to unconfirmed reports that the suspect was a member of the security forces and had recently formed part of the *Estado Mayor Presidencial*, the high-level security force which answers directly to the President.[57]

D. Torture and Murder of Street Children

Since the fall of 1989, Americas Watch and Physicians for Human Rights have received well-documented reports of violent abuses against Guatemala City's abandoned children who live on the streets in Guatemala City's Zone 1. While in the capital, our delegation met with forensic doctors, police investigators, and child welfare activists to learn what, if any, steps had been taken to identify and prosecute those responsible for these crimes.

Whether abuses directed against street children in Guatemala are new, or were simply underreported before, is unclear. In a highly unusual development, the aggressive pursuit of criminal cases against the suspected perpetrators by a U.S.-based children's group has resulted in convictions of police officers in two separate cases. Casa Alianza, the Guatemala City branch of the New York-based Covenant House, has launched legal proceedings against dozens of policemen for violent abuses against street children who are petty criminals or who have run afoul of the police in other ways. Unfortunately, as criminal cases have progressed, witnesses to the crimes and children's advocates have increasingly become targets of police vengeance as well.

---

[57] "Ordenan captura del presunto asesino de Myrna Mack Chang," *Siglo Veintiuno*, July 4, 1991.

The most recent of several threatening incidents against Casa Alianza occurred before dawn on July 18, 1991. Four armed men in a blue BMW with smoked glass windows drove by the Casa Alianza shelter in Zone 1 and shouted that they would kill Bruce Harris, Casa Alianza's Latin American director, and all of the shelter's staff and children. Minutes later, the car returned and the men opened fire on the shelter. Fortunately, no one was hurt.

Since it began documenting abuses against street children in March 1990, Casa Alianza has reported 14 cases of street children murdered by the police, 39 cases of torture or other violent abuse, and four disappearances. (Casa Alianza has also successfully presented 14 writs of *habeas corpus*, resulting in the release of minors from adult prisons.) In most of the cases reported, blame has fallen on the National Police, although the Treasury Police, and the combined patrol known as the Civilian Protection System (SIPROCI), which includes elements of the National Police, Treasury Police, and Mobile Military Police, have been responsible for abuses as well. Private security guards licensed by the National Police and the Interior Ministry have also committed violent abuses.

Casa Alianza estimates that 5,000 children live on the streets of the capital, principally in the city's Zone 1. Some were orphaned by political violence, others were abandoned by parents who had fled the country or were simply unable to support them. Some are the children of homeless parents. Many resort to petty crime to sustain themselves. Glue sniffing is common to relieve hunger and provide an escape from their difficult and precarious lives.

Many children are sent to closed rehabilitation centers in Guatemala City for periods of 45 days at a time for minor offenses. Our delegation received testimony of torture and ill treatment in the state-run detention center for girls, known as the Centro de Observación de Niñas Tom in Guatemala City's Zone 13. One girl who was twice sent to this center described being subjected to lengthy periods of isolation, submersion in a washtub of water to the point of near-drowning, and being forced to roll back and forth repeatedly over a floor covered with pebbles. The last two punishments, the girl said, were called *pila* and *rollo*, respectively. Children have also reported severe abuse at the government-run Hogar Rafael Ayau and the San José Pinula Reeducation Center, in the town of San José Pinula some twenty kilometers outside the capital, according to Casa Alianza.

Police Wipe Out the 18th Street Gang

In two separate incidents on June 5 and 15, 1990, eight youths who belonged to a gang based on 18th Street, in Zone 1 of the capital, were kidnapped by plainclothes police. One of the youths escaped, while four of the children's bodies were later discovered in a vacant lot in Mixco, a municipality just West of Guatemala City. Three more of the victims remain disappeared. Another member of the gang, 17–year–old Anstraum Villagrán Morales, was shot and killed by the police on June 25. We interviewed two witnesses to the June 5 kidnapping, including a girl who escaped after several hours' captivity and a boy who fled the scene, later to be captured and allegedly tortured by the police.[58] This witness, 17–year–old Gustavo Adolfo Cisneros (alias Toby), was himself stabbed to death on May 10, 1991, under circumstances which remain unclear. According to the witnesses, members of the gang had run afoul of the police in April 1990 after they robbed a colonel, his son, and a Treasury Policeman.

At about 10:00 a.m. on June 5, members of the gang were having a cup of *atol*, a drink made from cornflour, in front of a food stand on 18th Street, between 4th and 5th Avenues in the capital's Zone 1. A large black pickup truck with smoked glass windows drew up and four men emerged wearing cowboy hats and boots. All but one were wearing plaid shirts.[59] One man smacked 17–year–old gang member Gudiel Lizadro Melgar (alias Capitol) in the head with a pistol. When the witness, María Eugenia Rodríguez, 14, asked why he hit her friend, one of the men responded, "We have an account to settle with

---

[58] We also interviewed Casa Alianza staff and prosecutors from the Attorney General's office. National Police director Julio Caballeros declined to meet with our delegation. The deputy director scheduled a meeting with our delegation to be attended as well by police officers in charge of investigating abuses against street children and others. However this meeting was canceled abruptly without explanation and no alternative meeting time was offered. The cancellation may have been a result of police sensitivity on the issue provoked by the airing, the night before our scheduled meeting, of a documentary on the ABC–TV program Prime Time Live about police abuses of street children in Guatemala.

[59] The witness has told Casa Alianza that she saw one of the men accompanied by a uniformed police officer inside the headquarters of the National Police in Guatemala City on September 6.

you!" (*Ustedes están pendientes con nosotros.*) The men handcuffed four of the boys; the fifth, Toby, managed to run off. María Eugenia was not handcuffed, apparently because the men had only four pairs of cuffs. The four boys -- Capitol, Jovito Josué Castellanos (alias Canario), 17, Soruyo,[60] and Eduardo Salvador Sandoval (alias Catrachito), 16, and María Eugenia were thrown in the pickup truck.

Once they had their victims in the truck and, with the exception of María Eugenia, handcuffed, the men sprayed a liquid from a clear plastic bottle in their faces. Then the men placed a black bag filled with a pesticide known locally as Gamexane over the head of each child, one by one, causing them to lose consciousness. María Eugenia said that her eyes reddened and that she felt as if someone were pulling them out. Breathing became so difficult, she felt as if she were drowning. "Only it was worse," she said. Then, she noticed a bitter taste trickling down her throat before passing out.

María Eugenia awoke at about 3:00 p.m. The pickup truck had stopped inside the General Cemetery in Guatemala City's Zone 3. She saw three of the boys still sleeping in the truck with her. They looked badly bruised. The fourth boy, Capitol, was tied to a tree by his wrists, which were above his head. The men were beating him with a whip and demanding that he tell them "the truth." He was covered with blood. María Eugenia tried to wake up Canario, but he said he couldn't open his eyes because they were too heavy. She watched as her captors removed documents with mug shots of the kids from the truck. (She read the name of the police investigations department, DIC, on the papers.) They took the papers to a wooden tool shed and burned them. Again she tried to wake her friend Canario. He told her to run away. She sneaked out of the truck and escaped through a door in the wall of the cemetery. Outside she passed out again. She regained consciousness in the hospital, where she had been registered as intoxicated. It was then that she noticed little round

---

[60] There is some confusion as to the identity of the boy nicknamed Soruyo, whom María Eugenia said was kidnapped with her on June 5. Soruyo is a common nickname for a black child, as Catracho or Catrachito is for a Honduran. One of the youths found dead with other members of the 18th Street gang, Henry Geovanni Contreras, was called Soruyo. However, his mother told Casa Alianza he went missing on June 15, the date of the second group kidnapping.

marks on her left arm. The scars left by these marks, which looked like burns, were still visible at the time of our interview in mid-December.

The bodies of four of the kidnap victims —— Catrachito and Canario, who were kidnapped with María Eugenia on June 5, and Henry Geovanni Contreras (alias Soruyo), 17, and Luis Estuardo Piri Monterrozo, 17, who were seized on June 15 —— were found June 16 and 17 in a vacant lot in Mixco. Although the police report states that the bodies only bore gunshot wounds, photographs of the boys' faces show the signs of apparent torture. Dr. Kirschner reviewed enlargements of the police photographs of three of the youths and concluded that:

● Jorito Josué Castellanos had injuries on the right upper and lower eyelids in addition to a gunshot wound above the left eyebrow;

● Luis Estuardo Piri Monterrozo showed evidence of lacerations and abrasions around both eyes and on the forehead, with probable enucleation (removal) of the right eye, the photograph also showed bruising around both eyes and swelling of the nose, which may have been broken;

● Eduardo Salvador Sandoval showed a gunshot wound on the left eyebrow, hemorrhaging around both eyes, bruises on the lips, and injuries to the skin at the base of the neck, adjacent to the right eye, on the left cheek, and on the chin, which are consistent with chemical burns.

Casa Alianza filed criminal complaints for the murders and disappearances of members of the 18th Street gang. The agency also campaigned for international and national publicity regarding these and other abuses against street children. The pressure resulting from this publicity undoubtedly assisted in the prosecution of criminal cases and resulted in the National Police director instituting a series of weekly meetings with Casa Alianza to discuss its concerns in the second half of 1990.

On April 4, a judge issued arrest warrants for two policemen from Guatemala City's fifth precinct as well as a woman who works at the food stand from which the eight children were abducted. The policemen, Néstor Fonseca López and Samuel Rocail Valdez, and the woman, Rosa Trinidad Morales Pérez, are currently in pretrial detention. Although the suspects have been charged with the murder of Anstraum Villagrán, who police officers shot dead near the same food stall in June, the case has been combined with the judicial investigation into the kidnapping of the eight other members of the 18th Street gang, suggesting that the judge believes the same policemen were among those responsible.

A woman who works in the same food stall as Morales Pérez testified in court regarding the circumstances of the murder of Anstraum Villagrán, 17, on June 25. That day, Anstraum was drinking a beer at the stall and left to relieve himself. The two policemen now accused of his murder followed him between the stalls. Shortly thereafter, the woman heard two shots and saw the policemen run away. One of the agents is said to have been romantically involved with Morales Pérez, the woman currently being held in connection with the murder.

According to her co-worker, Morales Pérez threatened Anstraum on the day of his murder, saying he should be careful or he would be killed just like his companions. Morales is also suspected of having fingered the five street children kidnapped on June 5.

Two other members of the gang -- "Mish" and Toby -- were subsequently picked up and allegedly tortured in the National Police headquarters in the capital in separate incidents. We interviewed Toby, 17, who has lived on the street since his mother abandoned him to move to the United States ten years ago.

Toby was on 6th Avenue, in front of the "Capitol" movie theater in Zone 1, when four National Policemen approached him and asked if he knew Carlos Toledo, the coordinator of Casa Alianza's social workers, or "street educators." Toby denied knowing Toledo, to which one of the officers responded that he would kill him for lying. They handcuffed him and took him in a radio patrol car to the police headquarters. On the first floor, they blindfolded him. They took him to a small room on the third floor, where, he said, uniformed policemen tortured him for about two hours. They removed his shirt and blindfold and placed him in a metal barrel half-filled with water, which came up to his chest. Wires were attached to the tub and to switches on the walls, Toby said. Once he was inside the tub, the policemen turned on the electricity and four or five men pushed his head under water, he alleged. He felt his heart beating rapidly and afterwards felt dizzy and nauseated. The men took him out and put him back in the barrel four times, while asking him if he knew of a policeman who had killed a kid, which Toby falsely denied out of fear. They also asked if he used or sold drugs.

Toby told us of other incidents of threats and harassment he had suffered at the hands of the police. He also gave us the names of eleven of the original twenty members of the 18th street gang who had been murdered in the last seven months. He feared the police would kill him, too, he said.

Five months after our interview, on May 10, 1991, Toby was stabbed to death, apparently by another street child.

Convictions of Police in Two Cases

On March 4, 1990, four policemen attacked nine street children who had been sniffing glue in front of the "Electronics Xtra" store at the corner of 12th Street and 6th Avenue, in Zone 1 of the capital. The officers beat and kicked the children, pouring glue over some of them. A 13-year-old Salvadoran boy, Nahamán Carmona López, died in the hospital ten days later from the injuries inflicted by the police.[61]

On March 19, 1991, four National Police agents were convicted of murder in the case. The agents were sentenced to prison terms of 10 to 15 years, without parole. In addition, the four police agents were fined civil damages of 1–5,000 *quetzales* each ($200 – 1,000). According to the court's ruling, the sentences reflected a 25% increase because the homicide had been committed by police agents on official duty. Casa Alianza has appealed the sentencing, as Article 28 of the Guatemalan Penal Code requires a doubling of sentences when crimes against individuals or their property are committed by agents charged with maintaining public order. Simple homicide is punishable with eight to twenty years in prison, according to Article 123 of the Penal Code. Thus the police agents who murdered Nahamán Carmona López should have received a minimum of 16 years each.

On April 17, 1991, a conviction was obtained in the case of Marvin Oswaldo de la Cruz Melgar, a 13-year-old street child who was shot dead by police on May 22, 1990. According to the police, agent Gregorio Erasmo hit Marvin by accident while firing at a suspected thief.

---

[61] See Amnesty International, *Guatemala: Extrajudicial Executions and Human Rights Violations Against Street Children*, (London: July 1990), pp. 4 – 15.

51

Although the Fifth District Court in Guatemala City found two National policemen from the first precinct guilty; one of manslaughter (*homicidio culposo*) and the second of covering up the crime (*encubrimiento*), the agents were given suspended sentences of three years and freed on bail. Erasmo, the agent charged with manslaughter, was ordered to pay 2,000 *quetzales* (about $400) in civil damages and the other agent, Manuel Led González, 50 *quetzales* ($10). The father of the victim has appealed the ruling.

The conviction of police agents for the deaths of civilians is extremely rare in Guatemala, but not entirely unprecedented. As described in Chapter I, six policemen, including the departmental chief in Quezaltenango, were convicted for the kidnapping and murder of two university students in October 1987. However, the conviction was overturned on appeal. While the conviction of four policemen for the murder of Nahamán Carmona López is encouraging, it remains to be seen whether other convictions will follow.

At the same time, the convictions were won at a high cost. Witnesses in both cases suffered threats and persecution, threats which prompted a policewoman who testified against her colleagues in one case to flee into exile and a street child who witnessed the crime to go into hiding. Threats against a witness in the case of Marvin de la Cruz prevented him from appearing a second time in court to ratify his initial statement, thus weakening the evidence against the police. And finally, Casa Alianza's staff has increasingly suffered harassment, including threats, arrests on trumped up charges, and an attempted kidnapping. This persecution undoubtedly has resulted from Casa Alianza's unflagging advocacy for street children.

IV. THE MASSACRE AT SANTIAGO ATITLAN

Under a full moon on December 2, 1990, Guatemalan soldiers opened fire on thousands of unarmed Tzutujil Indians near the municipality of Santiago Atitlán. The Indians had gathered at the army stockade a mile from the town to protest the drunken behavior of four soldiers earlier that evening. As the shooting began, demonstrators in the front of the crowd threw themselves to the ground, while others ran into a grove of coffee trees across from the stockade. Thirteen people, including two children, died as a result of high velocity bullet wounds during or soon after the shooting, and twenty-three others were wounded. Eight days after the massacre, on December 10, our delegation interviewed several of the wounded who had been transported from Santiago Atitlán to the national hospital in Sololá. We also spoke with the hospital director, Dr. César Caballeros, and several of the physicians attending to the wounded. During their visit to Guatemala in January, Stover and Snow traveled to Santiago Atitlán where they, along with Father John E. Vesey, the Director of the Office of Human Rights/Human Life of the Diocese of Sololá, interviewed several witnesses, including the town mayor, Delfino Rodas Tobías, and visited the site where the massacre had taken place.

Background

Just over 45 miles west of Guatemala City, Lake Atitlán, with its lapis lazuli-blue waters shut in by purple highlands and olive green volcanoes, is one of the most beautiful lakes in the world. Tourists come here from around the world to admire the scenery and to buy handicrafts. But few are aware of the fear and death that have been a part of the region's history for the past decade.

What happened in the early morning of December 2 had been set in motion months, even years, before. The municipality of Santiago Atitlán is one of a dozen Indian communities, some named after the Apostles, that nestle on the shores of Lake Atitlán in the department of Sololá. Approximately ninety-six percent of Santiago Atitlán's 38,000 residents are indigenous and speak a Mayan dialect called Tzutujil. It is a deeply religious community, and nearly eighty percent of the town's inhabitants are Catholic. Most *Atitecos*, as the townspeople call themselves, are farmers who cultivate beans, corn, coffee, and fruits along the grassy slopes leading to the water.

The Army first established a presence in the department of Sololá in 1975, three years before the Organization of the People in Arms (OPRA) guerrilla organization was formed. In 1980, in response to increased guerrilla activity around the lake, the Army established a stockade in a hamlet called Panabaj on the outskirts of Santiago Atitlán. At the same time, two other garrisons were posted in the lakeside towns of Panajachel and San Lucas Tolimán. Since then, over 800 Atitecos have been killed or made to disappear by groups of heavily-armed men. On May 22, 1990, for instance, several hooded men reportedly forced passengers off of two buses just outside of town. They then pulled four men from the group and, as the passengers watched, began firing at the feet of their victims, as they moved their aim steadily higher.[62]

Atitecos blame the Army for much of the repression and violence that has plagued Santiago Atitlán for the past ten years. Soldiers typically vacate the town during the morning when the tourists descend from Panajachel, but by early evening, they return to keep a constant watch on the town's activities. For years now, residents of the town have observed a *de facto*, though not official, curfew between 10:00 p.m. and 4:00 a.m. Community leaders, catechists, and teachers have received death threats, prompting many to abandon their posts.[63] In 1987 alone, thirteen teachers left their jobs because of threats. In response, the National Teachers Union issued a statement in January 1988, charging the Army in Santiago Atitlán with "engaging in acts of intimidation against teachers and the general population."

Another source of tension between soldiers and residents of Santiago Atitlán are the civil patrols. In late 1987, military officers from the stockade threatened males with reprisals unless they reorganized the civil patrol. The townspeople, though reluctantly, reconstituted the civil patrol after several residents were killed or disappeared.

Residents have complained to local church and human rights groups that soldiers -- who the townspeople refer to as *kiks*, an Hispanicized Tzutujil term meaning "bloody ones" -- are often responsible for robberies in the town. During a recent robbery attempt, on November 20, 1990, neighbors in the hamlet of Xechiboy

---

[62] Robert Carlsen, "Report from Santiago," *Report on Guatemala*, Guatemala News and Information Bureau, Winter 1990, p. 4.

[63] See Americas Watch, *Closing the Space*, pp. 92–96.

caught two men breaking into a house. One of the men escaped and was later seen entering the stockade. The other would-be thief was turned over to the police, though he was subsequently released without charge or trial. From then on, the residents of Xechiboy decided to organize themselves against future robberies. They agreed that if there was a robbery being committed, the family in need would shout to their neighbors for help. The villagers, as a group, would then come to their aid.

The Massacre

On December 1, shortly before sunset, four army officers in civilian clothes arrived at a small *cantina*, or bar, located on the dirt road that connects Xechiboy with the stockade.[64] At least two of the men were armed with pistols. Inside the bar the men drank heavily and, an hour later, proceeded about fifty meters down the street where they entered another cantina, the Cevichería Luky. For about half an hour, the men abused and struck customers before staggering out onto the street where they continued to abuse passersby, threatening some of them with their firearms. At about 9:30 p.m., they returned to the Cevichería Luky, whose owner had closed and locked the door after their earlier visit. The soldiers banged on the door and shot their guns in the air. Hearing the gunshots, several armed soldiers left the stockade to investigate the disturbance.

An hour later, the soldiers, with their drunken comrades in tow, left the plaza in the direction of the stockade. But, en route, two of the men left the group and walked up a side street and then down a narrow alleyway to the house of a local resident, Andrés Sapacu Ajuchan. With their fists and boots, they pounded on his front door, shouting that they were members of the army and ordering Sapacu Ajuchan to come out. Fearing they were about to be kidnapped, Sapacu Ajuchan and his family called out for help. As Sapacu Ajuchan's neighbors rushed out of their houses, the two soldiers fled back down the street.

---

[64] The reconstruction of the events surrounding the massacre are based on interviews with witnesses conducted by mission delegates in December 1990 and January 1991. Also, see John E. Vesey, "Bloody Sunday: The Massacre in Santiago Atitlán," *America*, (forthcoming), and *Massacre in Santiago Atitlán*, a report of the Office of Human Rights of the Archdiocese of Guatemala, (Guatemala: December 1990).

Then someone hurled a stone, hitting one of the men in the head. Sapacu Ajuchan's neighbors captured one of the intruders just as his fellow soldiers were arriving to take him away. Meanwhile, the other intruder returned, pulled his pistol from his belt, and fired twice into the growing crowd, injuring an 18–year–old young man named Diego Ixbalán. In the ensuing turmoil, the soldiers liberated their captured comrade and returned immediately to the stockade.

After taking the injured boy to his house, the neighbors split into several groups: one group went to advise the National Police, another went to inform the mayor of Santiago Atitlán, while a third group went to the home of the President of the local committee of Catholic Action to borrow the keys to the church -- they would ring the church bells in order to summon other residents of the village.

The bells tolled for approximately one hour, from midnight until 1:00 a.m. Upon hearing the bells, many inhabitants thought that their priest had been killed. (Nine years earlier, on July 28, 1981, villagers had been roused from their sleep by the same sound and gathered in the plaza shortly after their pastor, Father Stan Rother of Oklahoma, had been murdered by four assailants.) Others thought that the church was on fire.

Thousands of people gathered in the plaza. At this moon–lit assembly, the people of Santiago Atitlán decided to march to the stockade to demand an explanation for the evening's earlier violence. Though reluctant at first, the mayor, Delfino Rodas Tobías, agreed to lead the march. He insisted, however, that the crowd go peacefully. As the mayor moved to the front of the crowd, several villagers gathered together white nylon sacks, fashioned them into flags, and tied them to sticks.

Over three thousand men, women, and children set out on the road from Santiago Atitlán to the stockade. On the way, the crowd stopped at the home of Diego Ixbalán. There, the newly elected mayor, Salvador Ramírez, joined Mayor Rodas Tobías at the head of the march.

As the crowd approached the darkened, sandbagged fortress, someone from inside called out on a megaphone: "What do you want? What's your problem? Go home! We'll resolve this in the morning!" Undeterred, the marchers, with the two mayors in the lead, advanced to within three feet from the entrance of the stockade, where several soldiers stood guard. In the *garitas*, or guardposts, both to the left and to the right of the guards, soldiers aimed machine guns at the crowd.

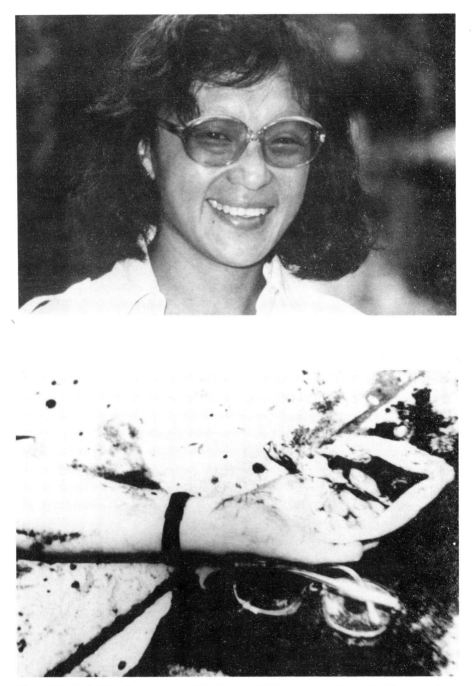

Myrna Mack's left hand grasps a possible ligature. This important piece of evidence was later discarded by police investigators.

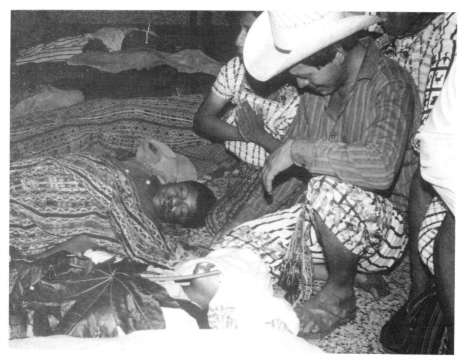

Relatives mourn family members who were gunned down in the massacre at Santiago Atitlán on December 2, 1990. (Photo: Peter Barwick)

Within ... of the massacre at Santiago Atitlán, the townspeople had placed crosses at the site bearing the ... mes of those who were killed. (Photo: Eric Stover)

Mission delegate Clyde Snow interviews Francisco Mendoza Teney, a thirteen-year-old boy who was wounded in the massacre at Santiago Atitlán. (Photo: Eric Stover)

As residents of San Antonio Sinaché look on, forensic investigators use archeological techniques to exhume an unmarked grave. (Photo: Eric Stover)

Clyde Snow directs the exhumation of an unmarked grave near the village of San Antonio Sinaché in December 1990. (Photo: Eric Stover)

The father of Sebastián Cos Morales stands next to his son's remains just exhumed from an unmarked grave. His son was executed by then local civil patrol chief, Delfino Pascual Hernández, in 1984. (Photo: Eric Stover)

Relatives and friends carry the remains of Sebastián Cos Morales and Pedro Tiniguar Turquiz. (Photo: Eric Stover)

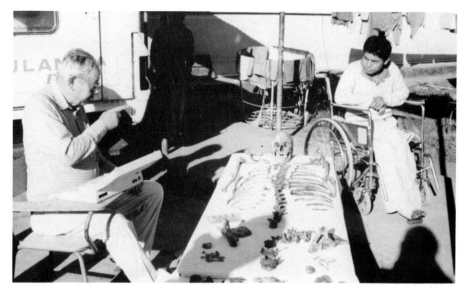

Clyde Snow examines the skeleton of Manuel Tiniquar Chitic in the hospital in Santa Cruz del Quiché. Snow determined that he had died from slashing blows to the back with an edged instrument. (Photo: Eric Stover)

This shirt with the wearer's skeletal remains still intact was exhumed in December 1990 from an unmarked grave in the Guatemalan highlands. Forensic anthropologist Clyde Collins Snow later determined that it belonged to Manuel Tiniguar Chitic, a farmer who was executed with his hands bound behind his back in 1984 by a local civil patrol chief. (Photo: Eric Stover)

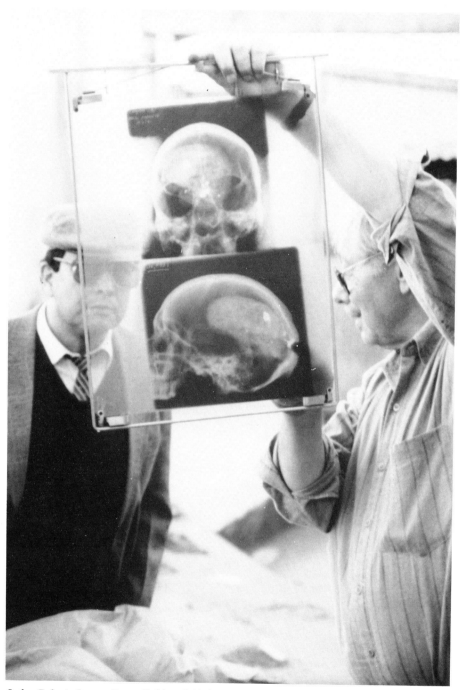

Judge Roberto Lemus Garza (left) and Clyde Snow examine X-rays of the skull of one of the two muder victims exhumed near San Antonio Sinaché in January 1991. The white spots on the X-rays are bullet fragments. (Photo: Eric Stover)

Seven years later, Pedro Tiniguar Turquiz's skull still bore the blindfold that was tied around his head shortly before he was shot and then buried in an unmarked grave. The beveled hole near the base of the skull is an exit wound. (Photo: Eric Stover)

Mayor–elect Salvador Ramírez spoke first. "Good morning," he said, "we would like to speak with your commander." Then, turning to the crowd, he added, "Please, quiet down, the mayor is going to speak." Taking a step toward the entrance, Rodas Tobías took off his red baseball hat. "Good morning," he said. At that moment, several gunshots rang out from inside the stockade. Immediately, soldiers in the two guardposts next to the entrance opened fire, aiming directly into the fleeing crowd. According to witnesses, at least one soldier left the stockade to shoot at the marchers. Several of the wounded say that they were shot while lying on the ground in front of the stockade. After the first gunshots, they hit the ground and, they say, the soldiers in the guard post above them opened fire, hitting several of them and killing some of their companions. One of the wounded says he survived because when he hit the dirt, two dead people fell on top of him. This witness later had to have a finger on his left hand amputated. In all, the shooting lasted three to five minutes, leaving 11 dead and 25 wounded (two of whom died later that day).

After the massacre, no medical personnel left the stockade to aid the wounded. Thus the survivors had to carry the injured in their arms to Santiago Atitlán. Hours later, the town's voluntary firemen arrived at the scene and transported the dead to the town hall. Among them were two children, aged ten and thirteen, who were fatally shot only a few paces away from the entrance to the stockade.

Another child, 13–year–old Francisco Mendoza Teney, later told us how he had been wounded. "I was toward the back of the crowd. When I heard the shots, I turned to flee through the coffee trees. But I ran into a barbed wire fence. I just hung there, unable to move. Then I felt a sharp pain in my left leg. I looked down and saw blood gushing out. That's when I passed out."[65] (Francisco's situation is especially tragic, as his father was kidnapped and killed by unidentified men six years ago. Soon thereafter, he left school in order to help his mother care for his three younger brothers. In January, Francisco was still in a body cast from the waist down.)

When dawn broke that morning, the wounded were ferried across Lake Atitlán to Panajachel and then transported by car to the national hospital in Sololá. The Army prohibits boats from crossing the lake at night, and anyone who makes a nighttime crossing is suspected of being a guerrilla. That delay proved fatal for two of the wounded. At

---

[65] Interview with Francisco Mendoza Teney in Santiago Atitlán, January 12, 1991.

the hospital, surgeons immediately operated on four of the most seriously injured -- only two of whom survived. Salvador Alvarado Sosof and Manuel Chiquita González died within hours of leaving surgery.

"I had a dilemma," one of the surgeons, Dr. Romeo Agustín Agustín, told us. "You see, I am one of only three surgeons in the department [of Sololá] and also its forensic doctor. When the injured arrived at the hospital, there were only two of us -- myself and the governor of the department, who is also a surgeon -- on duty. It was then that I learned that several people had died in Santiago Atitlán. So I phoned a local judge for advice. I told him that we had to operate right away, which meant I couldn't go across the lake to autopsy the dead. The judge told me the living were more important than the dead. So I stayed."

In the meantime, a public health worker in Santiago Atitlán examined the bodies externally and a justice of the peace issued death certificates, noting that they had all died of multiple gunshot wounds. Had the families wanted autopsies performed, they would have had to pay for transporting them across the lake to the morgue in the hospital in Sololá. As a result, no bullets were recovered and taken to the police ballistics lab in Guatemala City. Thus valuable evidence was lost regarding the types of weapons used and how many had been fired.

According to the office of the mayor of Santiago Atitlán, the following persons died in the massacre: Salvador Alvarado Sosof, Pedro Mendoza Pablo (29), Gaspar Coó Sicay (18), Juan Carlos Pablo Sosof (20), Pedro Mendoza Catú (18), Pedro Cristal Mendoza (13), Gerónimo Sojuel Sisay (10), Juan Ajuchán Mesía (17), Felipe Quiejú Culán (53), Salvador Damián Yaqui (50), Pedro Damián Vásquez (44), Nicolás Ajtujal Sosof (25), and Manuel Chiquita González (19).

Those wounded during the massacre were Antonio Pablo Toj (21), Gaspar Tzina Teney (16), Cristobal Tacaxoy (53), Antonio Chivilu Quiejú (45), Salvador Sisay Bablo (18), Antonio Reanda Coche (26), Nicolas Tziná Esquina (40), Pascual Mendoza Coché (15), José Sosof Coó (17), Francisco Mendoza Teney (13), Pedro Culan Sosof (39), Pedro Zapulu Xicay (30), Nicolas Ratzan Sapalu (25), Esteban Damián Coó Coquic (24), Gaspar Mendoza Mendoza (24), Mariano Tacaxoy Rodríguez (15), Diego Pablo Petzey, Diego Ajchomajay Coché, Pedro Abraham Damián González, Juan Ixbalán Tziná, and Diego Yaquí Coché.

As the hospital surgeons tried to save the lives of the wounded, Guatemala's human rights ombudsman, Ramiro de León Carpio, flew by helicopter from Guatemala City to Santiago Atitlán. That morning residents had set up tables on street corners and begun collecting signatures and thumbprints for a petition to be sent to President Cerezo. More than 20,000 residents signed the petition, which was presented to the ombudsman by Mayor Rodas Tobías. The petition requested that President Cerezo (1) immediately remove all Army personnel from Santiago Atitlán, (2) carry out a thorough and impartial investigation of the massacre, and (3) bring those responsible for the massacre to justice.

The Government's Response

On Monday, December 3, Colonel Gustavo Adolfo Méndez Herrera, the Sololá-based commander of the 14th Military Zone, told representatives of the Human Rights Office of the Archdiocese of Guatemala that his soldiers had only opened fire "in self defense" after several shots were fired toward the stockade. He blamed the shooting on members of a so-called secret guerrilla organization, the *Resistencia Popular Campesina*, or Popular Peasant Resistance, who, he alleged, had infiltrated the march and provoked the crowd to act violently.[66] According to Méndez, the group has about 640 members who maintain a climate of terror over the residents of Santiago Atitlán. One of the group's strategies, he said, is to cause confrontations between the civilians and soldiers.

Later in the week, the defense minister, General Juan Leonel Bolaños Chávez, announced that "as proof of the Armed Forces' goodwill" the soldiers at the stockade would be moved to another location by the beginning of the year.[67] He also announced the arrests of Lieutenant José Antonio Ortiz Rodríguez, garrison commander, and Sergeant Major Efraín García González, saying they were responsible for provoking the incident. The general also said that the military would try to determine who were the agitators that induced the population to confront the soldiers at the stockade.

---

[66] See Human Rights Office of the Archdiocese, *The Massacre in Santiago Atitlán*, pp. 7–8.

[67] See Lucy Hood, "Guatemala Apologizes for Killings," *Washington Post*, December 8, 1990.

"The armed institution is profoundly sorry for what happened in Santiago de Atitlán," Bolaños Chávez said. But he added that the Army "should not be condemned because of the irresponsible attitude of two of its members."

A day later, President Cerezo stubbornly insisted that "the Army has been respectful of constitutional rights, and now finds itself involved in a circumstance caused by the actions or errors of a few of its members; therefore, we must blame circumstances and individuals, not institutions."[68] He also asked Guatemalans to remember "that public demonstrations must be carried out between 0600 and 1800 because these types of incidents can occur."

In response to the Army's version of events, the human rights ombudsman, Ramiro de León Carpio, told reporters that "the error that [the Army] wants to commit now is graver than that committed on Sunday [December 2] in Santiago Atitlán, for now they want to change the version of how things happened." There was no mob, nor was it an uprising, the Ombudsman said. "The shots were not fired into the air, but rather were fired indiscriminately into the group of people," he added. The army must bring the matter to the courts as soon as possible, de León Carpio said.[69]

In its report, the Ombudsman's office called the massacre an "act of genocide." The killings, it said, "were without any justification, since there was no violence directed against members of the Guatemalan army." The report went on to say that the massacre "was a culmination of years of intimidation, abuses of authority...extrajudicial executions, and disappearances [in Santiago Atitlán] for which the Guatemalan army was responsible." Finally, the report said that two other officers should also have been arrested.[70]

In response, Col. Edgar Leonel Ortega Rivas, the newly appointed public relations chief for the Army, said, "Whoever says that there are more than two [soldiers] implicated is an enemy of the army."[71]

---

[68] "Cerezo Calls Massacre 'Tragic,'" *Siglo Veintiuno*, December 8, 1990, reprinted in *FBIS*, December 12, 1990, p. 12.

[69] "Ejército quiere cambiar versión," *Prensa Libre*, December 5, 1990.

[70] Informe del Procurador de los Derechos Humanos, Ref. Exp. E.I.O. Sololá 27-90/9, December 7, 1990.

[71] "Acusación contra el Procurador," *Prensa Libre*, December 12, 1990.

The Human Rights Office of the Archdiocese of Guatemala, in its report on the massacre, maintained that there was no provocation or shooting from the crowd, and held the Army wholly responsible for the killings. It also condemned the Army for failing to assist the wounded. In addition to the immediate removal of the stockade from Santiago Atitlán, it recommended that government indemnify the wounded and the families of those who died during and after the massacre. (On December 4, the National Congress adopted a resolution calling on the government "to provide economic compensation to the families affected by the massacre."[72])

The Aftermath

In January 1991, two members of our delegation -- Clyde Snow and Eric Stover -- travelled to Santiago Atitlán, along with Father John E. Vesey, to interview witnesses to the massacre. Walking through the town, we saw large black bows hanging as memorials to the dead above the doorways of homes and shops. In the Cathedral across from the main plaza, the townspeople had decorated the shrine to the slain priest Stan Rother with strips of colored papers bearing the names of hundreds of residents who had been kidnapped, tortured, or killed in recent years. To cope with these losses, survivors had formed support groups for the wounded and relatives of the dead.

At the time of our visit, the government of Guatemala had fulfilled only one of the requests made by the residents of Santiago Atitlán: in mid-December, the Army withdrew its garrison from the stockade in Santiago Atitlán. However, more than a month after the incident, neither the military nor the police had conducted an *in situ* investigation of the massacre. Nor had the military judge, Sara María Vides Figueroa, responsible for the Army's inquest, interviewed any of the eye-witnesses, including the two mayors who led the march. (Judge Vides is an *Auditor de Guerra*, or War Auditor, who, although a civilian, holds the rank of captain in the army.) Moreover, only two soldiers have been arrested in connection with the incident, even though demonstrators who were directly in front of the stockade say that up to as many as 15 soldiers opened fire. Seven months after the massacre, the military judge still has not interviewed any townspeople who witnessed the crime, nor has any soldier been formally charged.

---

[72] "Congress Condemns Massacre, Demands Investigation," *El Gráfico*, December 5, 1990, reprinted in *FBIS*, December 12, 1990, p. 11.

Equally disturbing is the fact that none of the families of the dead nor the wounded have received financial compensation.[73] At least 10 families have been deprived of breadwinners, and several others have been placed in extremely difficult economic situations because of severe injuries caused by the high velocity military ammunition.

By the time of our visit in mid-January, only one of the wounded, José Sosof Coó, aged 17, remained in hospital. José had been wounded in the back, near the lower spine, and his physicians feared without specialized orthopedic surgery and rehabilitation José could become paralyzed from the shoulders down. Together, Father John E. Vesey, Mrs. Chris Houk, and Clyde Snow made arrangements to have José, accompanied by his father, airlifted to the United States for medical care. On February 26, Jose was admitted to the Presbyterian Hospital in Oklahoma City. He was later sent to the O'Donaghue Rehabilitation Clinic where he entered a physical therapy program.

Several Guatemalans and Americans associated with the Diocese of Sololá and Catholic parishes in the Oklahoma City area donated their time and resources to facilitate José's trip to the United States. Once in Oklahoma City, he was provided free hospital care and treatment -- all of which was paid for by private donations.[74] This collaborative effort stands in stark contrast to the indifference that the Guatemalan government has shown towards the families of those who were wounded or killed in the massacre.

Given their limited resources, the Ombudsman's office, the Archdiocese of Guatemala, and the Diocese of Sololá carried out competent and impartial investigations of the events surrounding the massacre. They responded quickly, sending investigators to the scene to gather facts, and within days of the massacre had made their

---

[73] According to the "Principles on the Effective Prevention and Investigation of Extra-legal, Arbitrary and Summary Executions," adopted by the United Nations Economic and Social Council on May 24, 1989, "The families and dependents of victims of extra-legal, arbitrary and summary executions shall be entitled to fair and adequate compensation, within a reasonable period of time."

[74] Several Oklahoma churches, individuals, and institutions have assisted José and his father. Special recognition are due the staff of the O'Donoghue Rehabilitation Institute of the University of Oklahoma Health Sciences Center; David L. Dunlap, the President and Chief Executive Officer of HCA Presbyterian Hospital; and Andrew A. Lasser, Ph.D, the Chief Executive Officer of the Oklahoma Medical Center at the University of Oklahoma Health Sciences Center.

findings public. According to many Atitecos, Human Rights Ombudsman Ramiro de León Carpio's trip to Santiago Atitlán the same day as the massacre helped prevent further confrontations between the townspeople and the Army.

These preliminary efforts, however, do not relieve the Guatemalan government of its responsibility to conduct a thorough, impartial, and open investigation of the massacre and to bring all those responsible for this tragedy to justice.[75] The investigation should include the testimonies of survivors, as well as those of soldiers who participated in the massacre. Some of the questions that still need to be answered include:

- What type of weapons (and how many) were used during the shooting?
- How many soldiers fired upon the crowd?
- Who gave the orders, if any, for the soldiers to commence shooting?
- Did any of the soldiers, as witnesses claim, ever leave the stockade to fire at marchers who had fallen to the ground or sought refuge in the coffee plantation?
- Why did medical personnel at the stockade fail to come to the aid of the wounded?
- Was the drunken and abusive behavior of the four officers on the eve of the massacre an aberration or a pattern that had existed for years? And, if so, why were disciplinary measures never taken to stop it?
- Why after so many years of complaints by the townspeople hadn't the military or civilian authorities investigated reports that soldiers were responsible for robberies, disappearances, and killings in Santiago Atitlán?

The Guatemalan government has responded to the massacre in Santiago Atitlán by blaming individual soldiers rather than the Army as an institution. While it is important to single out those responsible for the killings and punish them, the civilian authorities would be disingenuous, if not blatantly dishonest, to ignore the fact that Army officers and soldiers have routinely abused the residents of Santiago

---

[75] See "Principles on the Effective Prevention and Investigation of Extra-legal, Arbitrary, and Summary Executions," adopted by the United Nations Economic and Social Council (Resolution 1989/65 of May 24, 1989).

Atitlán. Until the Guatemalan government takes measures to end these abuses in Santiago Atitlán and elsewhere, it will only dishonor the memory of those who marched and died that December night.

* * *

Last May, Guatemalan soldiers attempted on two occasions to return to Santiago Atitlán and were quickly rebuffed by the townspeople. They did it peacefully, relying on their sheer numbers to block the army patrols from entering the town.[76] The people carried no weapons; only whistles, the national flag, and a white flag of peace.

The first patrol was spotted by farmers early on the morning of May 23. Within hours, about 1,000 unarmed townspeople confronted the 40-man patrol. A standoff ensued. At midday, the provincial governor, the local representative of the national human rights office, and a judge arrived to mediate. Three hours later, the officers of the patrol signed an agreement to leave and not return.

The next day, May 24, two Army patrols from another base arrived in the nearby village of Mirador. This time an even larger group of Atitecos confronted the troops. After three hours of dialogue, the soldiers agreed to leave.

---

[76] See David Clark Smith, "Guatemalan Town Insists It's Still Off-Limits to Army," *Christian Science Monitor*, May 30, 1991.

V. DIGGING UP THE PAST
THE GRAVES AT SAN ANTONIO SINACHE

Between 1970 and 1986, tens of thousands of Guatemalans disappeared or were murdered for political reasons. During the regime of Major General Fernando Romeo Lucas García (1978–1982), hundreds of people were killed every month, most of them by officially sanctioned death squads. In the counterinsurgency campaigns of the early 1980s, army troops under the command of President General Efraín Ríos Montt continued the carnage by destroying hundreds of villages. This grim legacy has left hundreds – – perhaps thousands –– of unmarked graves hidden in the fields and valleys of the highlands of Guatemala.

In recent years, the Mutual Support Group, the organization of the relatives of the disappeared, has obtained information on the existence of more than 100 clandestine cemeteries in Guatemala.[77] Most of them are located in areas where government–sponsored killings were particularly widespread in the early 1980s. GAM and other human rights groups have petitioned the courts to exhume graves at seventeen separate sites. By March 1991, however, only eight exhumations had been carried out.

"All of us in GAM support exhumations," GAM's president Nineth Montenegro de García told our delegation. "They are important for psychological and moral reasons. Not knowing where our loved ones are slowly eats away at us. It is better to know that they killed our relatives, as difficult as that is to accept, than to live with the pain of not knowing where they are."

GAM and other groups, such as the CERJ, believe that establishing the fate of the disappeared and bringing those responsible for their deaths to justice are necessary steps for promoting greater respect for human rights in Guatemala. An important part of this process is the exhumation, identification, and determination of the cause and manner of death of the disappeared. From a humanitarian point of view, families will finally know the fate of their loved ones and be able to give them a proper burial. In addition, through forensic documentation and subsequent litigation, the knowledge that those responsible for such crimes can be held accountable for their actions,

---

[77] See Amnesty International, *Guatemala –– Lack of Investigations into Human Rights Abuses: Clandestine Cemeteries*, (London: March 1991) (AMR 34/10/91), p. 3.

may deter political killings in the future both in Guatemala and elsewhere.

These groups also want to chronicle the fate of the disappeared for the historical record by preserving both anecdotal and physical evidence. One of the ways to suppress a people is to alter or destroy their identity. And one of the ways to destroy their identity is to change their history -- to make people disappear, to bury them in anonymous graves, and then to deny that such events ever took place. This is unforgivable. It is an attempt not only to distort history but also to erase part of the cultural history of Guatemala's indigenous population.

Military authorities in Guatemala have dismissed the clandestine cemeteries as simply the burial grounds of guerrillas killed in combat by the army or civil patrols. In 1988, then Minister of Defense General Héctor A. Gramajo explained the unmarked graves, asserting that "[Civil patrol] members always buried their dead legally, while insurgents did just the opposite....subversives buried their dead companions clandestinely without telling villagers the location of these burial sites."[78]

For relatives of the disappeared, obtaining an exhumation order can be time-consuming and dangerous. Many of them have had their efforts obstructed by the courts, and have faced delays of up to five months in the processing of requests for exhumations. Others have been threatened with death.

On August 26, 1988, the civil patrol chief in the village of Pachoj, El Quiché department, threatened to kill Juan Ajanel Pixcar and Sebastiana Ramos, both GAM members, for their role in pressing for the exhumation of three relatives allegedly killed by patrol members in the early 1980s and exhumed in June 1988.[79] The threats were made during a meeting called by the village's auxiliary mayor, ostensibly to discuss elections for a new mayor. The military commissioner and several civil patrollers allegedly responsible for the killings were also present at the meeting. According to GAM, the commissioner was concerned that Ajanel Pixcar and Ramos would be able to provide direct proof of his responsibility for the killings.

On two separate occasions in 1988, civil patrollers in the village of Pacoc, El Quiché, tried to abduct Juana Calachij, a member of the

---

[78] See Amnesty International, *Guatemala -- Lack of Investigations*, p. 4.

[79] See Amnesty International, "Guatemala: Death Threats Against Relatives of Victims of Extrajudicial Killings," September 14, 1988 (AMR 34/24/88).

Coordinadora Nacional de Viudas de Guatemala (CONAVIGUA), National Coordinating Committee of Guatemala Widows, for her role in arranging the exhumation of five bodies from a mass grave earlier in the year. One of the victims was her husband, Pedro de la Cruz, who, along with four other men, was allegedly hacked to death with machetes by patrollers in May 1984. Civil patrollers continue to watch Calachij's movements and, in June 1990, attempted to abduct her a third time.

Despite such threats, relatives of the disappeared have succeeded in obtaining several court–ordered exhumations. Between February 1988 and November 1990, sixty–four skeletons were exhumed from six clandestine cemeteries in the highlands of Guatemala. All of the cemeteries were located in El Quiché department.[80] Of the sixty–four sets of remains, only eight (12.5 percent) have been identified. Relatives identified the deceased from clothing remnants, particularly belts and shoes, or other artifacts such as jewelry. Nineth Montenegro de García recalls the scene at the exhumation of five bodies from a common grave in the village of Pacoc, El Quiché department, in June 1988:

> All of us worked at unearthing that grave –– the relatives, the firemen, even children. Little by little, we found bones and pieces of clothing. Some of the bodies were identified simply on the basis of the belts they were wearing. But the bones were all mixed together, so the forensic doctor couldn't match the bones anatomically. I still have my doubts about the identifications because it was all so rudimentary. It was terrible, the children were crying, and relatives were pointing and saying, 'That's him, that's him'...Eventually the forensic doctor began stacking bones and bits of clothing in a pile beside

---

[80] According to information collected by GAM and CERJ, and later published by Amnesty International, two other clandestine cemeteries were excavated in 1989. One was located in Monte Bello, Chimaltenango and another in Santa Rosa Chujuyub, El Quiché. However, no bodies were found at these sites, except for a toebone at Santa Rosa Chujuyub. Exhumations have been requested at nine other sites in the departments of El Quiché, Alta Verapaz, and Chimaltenango.

the grave and saying, 'Okay, this is so and so.' Then the relatives put the remains in separate plastic bags and took them away.[81]

GAM is concerned that, in an effort to prevent further investigations, the military and civil patrollers under their command may be removing evidence from the clandestine graves. For instance, in June 1989, when an exhumation team arrived at the site of a secret burial in Santa Rosa Chujuyub, El Quiché department, they found that the earth around the site had been recently disturbed. However, an excavation was carried out and a human toe bone was found. In May 1991, Americas Watch was informed by a credible source who requested anonymity that the army, when it learned that the courts were investigating the common grave in Santa Rosa Chujuyub, had ordered civil patrollers to dig up the remains and remove them to another place. Army personnel in plain clothes then observed the court-ordered exhumation, according to the source.

Many exhumations in Guatemala have been carried out without any attempt to determine the cause and manner of death of those exhumed, even though government authorities in both the Cerezo and Serrano administrations have stated publicly that they are committed to establishing the truth about the fate of the disappeared. For instance, in March 1990, then Minister of the Interior, General Carlos Morales Villatoro, told the press: "[I]t is important to find the truth in these cases, and this is why we are asking the victims' relatives to provide the necessary data to find the truth. These events happened eight years ago...and at the same time they concern us and oblige us to investigate them, so that there is a possibility that many families may know of the fate of the relatives who disappeared in the past."[82]

Apart from vague public statements, Guatemala's civilian authorities have lacked the political will to undertake serious medicolegal investigations of the disappeared. As a result, the task has been left to the relatives of the missing who must petition a judge for an exhumation. This unfairly places the burden on relatives for what is really the responsibility of governments: to investigate and prosecute serious crimes.

---

[81] Interview, Guatemala City, December 7. 1990.

[82] Quoted in Amnesty International, *Guatemala -- Lack of Investigations*, p. 2.

This situation is further compounded by the fact that forensic doctors in Guatemala, like most forensic pathologists in the United States and elsewhere, have never received training in forensic anthropology. Nor are there any forensic anthropologists in Central America, let alone Guatemala, who judges can call on to aid them in their investigations.

A. Disinterment and Analysis of Skeletal Remains

Forensic anthropologists are physical anthropologists who specialize in the scientific disinterment and analysis of skeletal remains and apply that knowledge to civil and criminal investigations. Few anthropologists, perhaps no more than sixty, practice forensic anthropology in the world.[83] Fewer still have ever used their skills to expose atrocities committed by governments.

In most medicolegal investigations of skeletal remains, the forensic anthropologist sets out to establish the identity of the deceased and to determine the time, cause, and manner of death. This is often a collaborative effort in which the forensic anthropologist functions as a member of a multidisciplinary team consisting of pathologists, odontologist, and other forensic specialists. In the United States, such a team usually works under the direction of the coroner or state medical examiner. In Guatemala, it would function under the direction of each department's forensic doctor.

Any medicolegal investigation of buried remains begins with an excavation of the burial site.[84] So as not to lose vital evidence, the excavation must be handled with the same exacting care given a crime scene search. In some cases, it is necessary first to locate the grave. This is usually done by removing all undergrowth and scraping away the topsoil. Graves appear lighter than the surrounding ground because the darker topsoil has mixed with the lighter subsoil in the grave fill.

Once the outline of the grave has been established, the exhumation team, under the direction of a forensic anthropologist, digs a test probe at the foot of the grave to determine the level of the burial. With this

---

[83] See Clyde C. Snow, "Forensic Anthropology," *Annual Review of Anthropology*, 1982; 11:97–131.

[84] See "Model Protocol for Disinterment and Analysis of Skeletal Remains," Appendix D.

established, the dirt over the grave can be removed with picks and shovels to a level of ten centimeters above the skeleton. After the overburden, as the surface soil is called, has been removed, the team begins meticulously removing the dirt with trowels and soft brushes until the complete skeleton is exposed. It is then photographed, and taken to the morgue for laboratory study.

Such a methodical approach pays dividends in the recovery of many small and fragile items such as teeth, bullets, and personal effects which are often critical in the identification of the victim and determination of the cause and manner of death. Moreover, special studies of the delicate remains of plants and insects found in the grave can aid in establishing the time of death.

In most cases, antemortem dental or medical X-rays provide the most immediate means of identifying skeletal remains. If, for one reason or another, sufficient radiological evidence is not available, the forensic anthropologist will undertake an anthropological study of the skeleton. Such a study involves determining the skeleton's age at death, sex, race, stature, and handedness. This information is then compared with the deceased's antemortem characteristics to see if they match. For instance, the handedness of a skeleton can often be determined by examining the surface of the shoulder joint of the scapula, or shoulder blade. Regularly extending the arm can change the shape of the bone, and a lifelong preference of one arm over the other -- handedness, in the anthropological vernacular -- would be noticeable. In addition, using one arm more often causes the bones of that arm to grow longer, sometimes by several millimeters. Thus if a skeleton and the person in life are found to be left-handed -- a trait found in only about 15 percent of the population -- the odds that they are one and the same are greatly increased. Similarly, old diseases and injuries often leave their traces on the skeleton, providing evidence for positive identification.

Through a combination of training and experience, forensic anthropologists are able to distinguish between various types of trauma to the bone which the inexperienced eye may fail to detect. Signs of violent death on the skeleton vary from the grossly obvious such as massive blunt force trauma or bullet holes in the skull to easily overlooked minor cuts or nicks by a fatal stab wound. Even strangulation can leave its mark on the bone: ligature or manual strangulation often result in the fracture of the hyoid bone, a small and delicate U-shaped bone located at the root of the tongue, which is seldom recovered unless the grave is carefully excavated.

B. Manuel Tiniguar Chitic

On November 8, 1990, a month before our delegation arrived in Guatemala, a 28-year-old farmer named Manuel Cos Morales appeared at the regional office of the human rights ombudsman in Santa Cruz del Quiché. Cos Morales was from San Antonio Sinaché, a mountain village belonging to the municipality of Zacualpa. He had come to the ombudsman's office to file a complaint against one of his neighbors, Delfino Pascual Hernández.

According to Cos Morales, in 1984, when Hernández was chief of the civil patrol in the village, he killed four of his fellow patrollers and had their bodies buried in separate graves near the village. One of the men was the complainant's younger brother, Sebastián. The others were Manuel Tiniguar Chitic, Pedro Tiniguar Turquiz, and Juan Toj Aguilar. Now, six years later, Cos Morales and his neighbors wanted the graves exhumed and Hernández arrested for murder.

We first learned of Cos Morales's complaint during an interview with the auxiliary ombudsman for the Department of El Quiché, Oscar Cifuentes Cabrera, on December 10, 1990. Later that day, in a meeting with Judge Roberto Lemus Garza and the department's forensic doctor, Ana Lisette García de Crocker, we discussed the possibility of excavating one of the three graves. Clyde Snow, it was decided, would use the exhumation to train Dr. García de Crocker and her assistant, Flavio Montúfar Dardón, in the scientific methods and techniques used to disinter and analyze skeletal remains.

On the morning of December 13, Snow and another member of our delegation, Eric Stover, met with their forensic colleagues and Judge Lemus Garza in Santa Cruz del Quiché and drove to San Antonio Sinaché. Mark Epps, a British volunteer with CERJ, joined the group to videotape the exhumation.[85]

Upon arriving in San Antonio Sinaché, Snow and his team were met by Manuel Cos Morales and several men in front of a white-washed adobe church. From its steps one could see the pine covered hills surrounding the village. Here and there, charred houses, the remnants of the army's scorched earth campaign of the 1980s, were visible on the slopes.

As a young boy rang the church bell, calling everyone to the village, Cos Morales led the group past the community *pila*, or well,

---

[85]The video is available for teaching purposes. For more information, contact Americas Watch at (202) 371-6592.

to a grove of bananas. Near the center of the grove, he paused to confer with his companions and then pointed to the ground. Manuel Tiniguar Chitic was buried here, he said. As for the other three men, their bodies were buried at least two kilometers away from the village.

Using machetes and large, razor-sharp hoes, the men cleared the undergrowth away from the grave. Snow then instructed them to use their hoes carefully to skim away the overburden. Within an hour they hit bone. Manuel Tiniguar Chitic's mother, sobbing loudly, watched as the contours of the skeleton slowly emerged. It lay face down in the grave, arms bound behind the back, fully clothed in a red shirt, blue trousers, and black leather shoes. Lying next to it was a *morral*, a typical cloth bag used by Quiché men.

Nearly the entire village turned out for the exhumation. Some volunteered their help. Others stood for hours at the edge of the banana grove watching as Snow and his team labored over the grave. A group of villagers whispered nervously when several men said to be civil patrollers suddenly appeared next to the pila. But they soon left.

As Snow and the team removed the bones and clothing from the grave and placed them in a large wooden box, Judge Lemus Garza gathered the villagers in front of the church. Speaking through a Quiché interpreter, he asked if they had any objections to the remains being taken to Santa Cruz del Quiché for further study. There were none. He then asked for eye-witness accounts of how Tiniguar Chitic had died.

The crowd grew quiet. A minute passed before several men spoke up. They had to be careful, one of them said, because Delfino Pascual Hernández lived only a few hundred meters away. He owned a rifle and, though he was no longer the patrol chief, a group of patrollers -- most of whom were members of the military reserve -- were loyal to him. Two months earlier, after army troops had temporarily moved into the village, Pascual Hernández's gang began threatening to kill those men who refused to participate in the patrol. That was why the village had sent Cos Morales into Santa Cruz del Quiché to file the complaint.

No one could recall the exact date of Manuel Tiniguar Chitic's death. But they were sure it had taken place during one of the months after Easter 1984. Earlier that year, Tiniguar Chitic had left San Antonio Sinaché to work in the sugar cane fields on the Pacific Coast. One morning after his return to the village, he was captured by Pascual Hernández and taken to the church. The bell was tolled, and everyone gathered near the pila.

Pascual Hernández denounced Tiniguar Chitic as a "traitor" and "subversive" for having missed his *turno*, or tour of duty, as a civil patroller.[86] He told the patrollers to tie him to a tree and ordered them, including several members of Tiniguar Chitic's family, to beat him with machetes and sticks. Witnesses said he was struck nearly twenty times before he collapsed. Then, with his hands still bound behind his back, he was carried to the banana grove and thrown face down into the hastily dug grave.

Back in Santa Cruz del Quiché, Snow spent two days with Dr. García de Crocker and her assistant, Montúfar Dardón, poring over the bones and clothing. He showed them how to determine sex, race, stature, handedness, and age at death by studying certain key features in the skeleton. He found that the skeleton belonged to a right-handed, American Indian male who was roughly 5'5" tall and approximately 35 years old, plus or minus seven years, and that the skull was missing two mandibular first molars -- all characteristics belonging to Manuel Tiniguar Chitic. The deceased, Snow concluded, had died from slashing blows to the back with an edged instrument.[87]

C. Sebastián Cos Morales and Pedro Tiniguar Turquiz

In mid-January 1990, Clyde Snow and Eric Stover, at the request of Judge Lemus Garza, returned to Guatemala to exhume two more unmarked graves near San Antonio Sinaché. In addition to the original team, the judge invited four of his colleagues, as well as several CERJ staff members including the organization's president,

---

[86] The frequency and number of hours which men must patrol depends on how much manpower is available in a given town or village. In some larger towns, the patrol goes out once every two months for twelve hours. But in smaller towns men are required to perform patrol duty once every three days for 24 hours or even 48 hours at a time. See Americas Watch, *Civil Patrols in Guatemala*, (New York: August 1986), pp. 51-52.

[87] In his report to Judge Lemus Garza, dated January 4, 1991, Snow gives the cause of death as follows: "The multiple cutting fractures observed in the lower thoracic and upper lumbar would have undoubtedly been associated with severe soft tissue injuries in this region. Assuming these were produced by multiple slashing blows from an edged instrument, it is highly likely they resulted in complete transection of the spinal cord and transverse lacerations of the abdominal aorta and inferior vena cava. The most likely immediate cause of death would have been through hypovolemic shock consequent to the massive hemorrhage."

Amílcar Méndez Urízar, to observe the exhumations.   Several policemen also accompanied the group.

According to villagers, the graves contained the remains of Sebastián Cos Morales and Pedro Tiniguar Turquiz.   In 1984, Cos Morales, 20, was patrol chief and Tiniguar Turquiz, 47, was his third–in–command.   Early that year, they had begun harassing Pascual Hernández to serve in the patrol, as was required of all the men in the village.   As a former member of the military reserve, Pascual Hernández claimed that he was exempt from patrol duty.[88] Eventually, Pascual Hernández went to the army base in Zacualpa, where he allegedly denounced the two men as guerrillas.   The army gave him a .22 caliber rifle and appointed him as the new patrol chief. Soon after his return to the village, he gathered several members of the patrol together and set out to capture his two antagonists.

He found them in a patrol hut about 2 kilometers from the village. It was midday on May 28.   The hut sat perched on a hill next to the foundation of a small church that had been burned to the ground during an army sweep two years earlier.   Behind the hut, on the hill's northern slope, was a bean field with a stream running through it. The two men, unarmed and apparently aware that Pascual Hernández was looking for them, had taken refuge in the hut.

By now, over 200 civil patrollers had gathered on the hill.   They watched as Pascual Hernández marched the two men out of the hut, blindfolded them, and forced them at gunpoint to lie face down in the field.   He then lowered his rifle and shot them twice through the left side of the head.   As the crowd dispersed, he ordered several patrollers to stay behind to bury the bodies.

Snow and his team found the two unmarked graves about five yards away from the stream.   They split into two groups.   Using the techniques he had learned at the earlier dig, Montúfar Dardón and another forensic assistant began exhuming the grave belonging to Pedro Tiniguar Turquiz, while Stover and Snow excavated another. As they worked throughout the day, villagers, including the families of both of the deceased, gathered on the hillside in the hot sun.

At one point, an elderly woman approached the group and introduced herself as Dominga Riguiac Cac.   Army soldiers, she said, had shot her husband, José Nas León, on February 14, 1981, while he was herding cows on the opposite side of the river.   She led the group

---

[88] This account is based on interviews with nine eye–witnesses, in San Antonio Sinaché, on January 9, 1990.

to where he was buried. It was agreed a team would return at a later date to exhume the grave.

After photographing Cos Morales's skeleton *in situ*, Stover and Snow began removing the bones. Cradling the mandible in one hand and the cranium in the other, Snow lifted Cos Morales's skull from the grave. Not only did he find that the blindfold was still firmly in place, but as he tilted the skull downward, a deformed .22 caliber bullet fell to the ground.

That was enough for Judge Lemus Garza. He immediately dispatched the policemen to apprehend Pascual Hernández at his house near the village. However, two hours later, they returned, empty-handed. The former patrol leader had fled, possibly as far away as Mexico, they said.

In the meantime, Flavio A. Montúfar Dardón had exposed the second skeleton. It also bore a blindfold in the form of a knotted handkerchief. When Montúfar Dardón showed relatives a white-metal ring with a small green stone which he had found on one of the finger bones of the left hand, they immediately identified it as Pedro Tiniguar Turquiz's wedding ring.

In his report to Judge Lemus Garza, Snow noted that both skeletons shared "certain significant features in common. Both were found in unmarked graves situated within a few meters of each other. Both crania were found with blindfolds still in place and both died from two closely-spaced, small-caliber (probably .22 long rimfire bullets) fired into the left side of the head. These findings suggest a common *modus operandi* and, perhaps, a single perpetrator." (See Appendix B.)

D. Future Exhumations

The exhumations at San Antonio Sinaché were relatively simple compared to ones which may be done in the future in which the identities of the deceased and the exact circumstances of the cause of death may not be known. For example, an exhumation of a clandestine cemetery has been scheduled to begin at this writing in the village of Chontalá, in the municipality of Chichicastenango in El Quiché department. The cemetery is said to contain the bodies of more than 100 victims slain in 1982. No information has yet been collected about the identities of the victims or the circumstances of their deaths. By contrast, dozens of villagers provided eye-witness testimony regarding the murders and subsequent burials of the three men at San Antonio Sinaché. The forensic analysis of the remains served to confirm their identities and support testimonial evidence regarding the cause and manner of death. Moreover, unlike cases of disappeared people where the bodies in question could belong to those of hundreds or even thousands of people, there was no need to search through the antemortem records of scores of people to find sets that matched the three skeletons.

Nonetheless, the exhumations at San Antonio Sinaché were instructive for several reasons. First, the investigators were able to recover several bullets and bullet fragments that can now serve as court evidence. In previous exhumations in Guatemala such items were usually lost because of improper excavation procedures.

Second, photographic evidence of the exposed skeletons *in situ* confirmed the eye-witness accounts of the murders at San Antonio Sinaché. This was particularly true in the case of Manuel Tiniguar Chitic, whose skeleton was found face down in the grave, with its hands bound behind the back. Such contextual evidence is usually lost when untrained workers use shovels and picks to excavate burials.

Finally, unlike previous exhumations in Guatemala where the callous mishandling of the remains by workers drew angry protests from relatives, the exhumations at San Antonio Sinaché were conducted in a manner that received the support of family members and villagers alike. This was due in large measure to the scientific method used in excavating the graves. In addition, the exhumation team took care to inform relatives of the procedures and to ask their permission to transport the remains to the city morgue for laboratory study.

On May 24, 1991, Dr. García de Crocker and Flavio Montúfar Dardón returned to San Antonio Sinaché to exhume two more unmarked graves. One belonged to Juan Toj Aguilar, the fourth murder victim mentioned in Manuel Cos Morales's complaint. His remains showed signs of extensive trauma from a sharp-edged weapon, possibly a machete. The other grave belonged to José Nas León. A gunshot wound to the head had shattered the skull into dozens of pieces.

To date, Pascual Hernández has not been arrested and is believed to be in hiding.

VI. THE ROLE OF THE UNITED STATES

After the Carter Administration's human rights policy brought a distancing between the United States and Guatemalan governments, the Reagan Administration was eager to warm relations with the Guatemalan military. Its many efforts to provide the army with aid, however, were rebuffed by the U.S. Congress until the military began moving towards allowing elections for a civilian government in 1985. Nonetheless, the Reagan Administration approved licenses for commercial sales of military equipment worth $769,800 between 1982 – 1985, despite legislation prohibiting the granting of export licenses for military equipment to governments "engaged in a pattern of gross violations of internationally-recognized human rights."[89] A program of military training was also launched in 1985 and provision of "nonlethal" military equipment –– i.e. not including arms and ammunition –– began to be provided the following year.

In addition, the Reagan Administration consistently whitewashed the Guatemalan security forces' horrendous human rights record in its annual *Country Reports on Human Rights Practices* and by means of public statements by high officials, including President Reagan.

The picture became more complex with the inauguration in Guatemala of Christian Democrat Vinicio Cerezo in 1986. Cerezo had close friends in the U.S. Democratic Party and won support from key lawmakers by virtue of his government's "active neutrality" regarding the *contra* war –– which the Reagan Administration supported and most Democrats opposed –– in Nicaragua. While winning him favor among Democrats, "active neutrality" won Cerezo the hostility of the Reagan Administration.   This dynamic explains the unusual phenomena which occurred for several years hence in which the Democrat-controlled Congress approved greater levels of military aid than that requested by the administration for Guatemala.

The Bush Administration, particularly since the arrival in Guatemala of U.S. Ambassador Thomas Stroock in 1989, has publicly criticized the Guatemalan authorities for human rights abuses, issuing scathing indictments in the *Country Reports on Human Rights Practices* in 1990 and 1991. In March 1990, Ambassador Stroock was recalled to Washington to protest a wave of political killings and

---

[89] Americas Watch and the British Parliamentary Human Rights Group, *Human Rights in Guatemala During President Cerezo's First Year*, (New York: February 1987), p. 89.

the government's failure to investigate them. And on December 21, 1990, the administration announced that it would suspend delivery of military aid and licensing of commercial arms sales to protest human rights violations, in particular the failure to investigate and punish those responsible for the June 1990 murder of U.S. citizen Michael Devine. Ambassador Stroock has interceded with Guatemalan authorities on several human rights cases, and apparently was responsible for the release from unacknowledged police detention of two Casa Alianza social workers in January 1991. Ambassador Stroock's statements and actions have raised the profile of human rights concerns in Guatemala, an important achievement in a country whose military considers the notion of human rights to be a communist invention.

The tables have turned in the U.S. Congress as well. With the end of the contra war in Nicaragua, liberals no longer feel the need to reward Guatemala for staying on the sidelines. At the same time, Guatemala's new president, Jorge Serrano, a conservative who served in the government of military dictator Efraín Ríos Montt, does not have friends among Democrats, as Cerezo did. Finally, there is a growing recognition that elections in Guatemala have not tempered the human rights behavior of the army and police. These factors have contributed to bringing about the first serious attempt by the Congress to limit aid to Guatemala on human rights grounds since civilians came into office.

The House Foreign Affairs Committee voted on May 23, 1991, to ban all military aid to Guatemala for fiscal years 1992 and 1993, except for aid to help demobilize combatants and monitor any ceasefire that might be produced by ongoing U.N.-brokered talks between the government and the guerrillas. The Committee also barred the commercial sale of weapons, ammunition, or armed aircraft to Guatemala. Moreover, the Committee placed strict limits on the use of Economic Support Funds (ESF), the most financially significant portion of U.S. aid. Since the advent of civilian government in 1986, Washington has provided hundreds of millons of dollars in ESF -- cash used mostly for payments of oil imports and debt financing. ESF totalled $56 million in fiscal 1990 and $30 million in fiscal 1991, although some $30 million in the 1990 allotment has been suspended for Guatemala's failure to meet economic policy criteria. The House Foreign Affairs Committee voted to limit all economic assistance to specific projects in areas such as fighting poverty or improving the environment, strengthening democratic institutions, or promoting fiscal reform, as opposed to balance of payments support. The restrictions on economic assistance could be waived if President Bush reports to Congress that Guatemala "has made progress in eliminating human rights violations and in investigating and bringing to trial those responsible for major human rights cases..."

The Bush Administration lobbied hard to prevent the Committee from adopting the restrictions, particularly against the effort to condition ESF on human rights performance. The end result reflected a compromise between the Administration's position and tougher restrictions which had been drafted by the Western Hemisphere Subcommittee. Report language subsequently passed by the Foreign Operations Subcommittee of the House Appropriations Committee is consistent with the Foreign Affairs Committee version. Approval by the full House and the Senate is necessary before the restrictions will become law.

VII. OBSERVATIONS AND RECOMMENDATIONS

A. Military and Economic Aid

• *Americas Watch and Physicians for Human Rights oppose resumption of military aid or the provision of economic support funds to the Government of Guatemala until it has stopped killings, torture, and disappearances by the security forces and taken concrete steps toward prosecuting those responsible for these crimes.* In this regard, both organizations view the amendment to the Foreign Assistance Authorization passed by the House Committee as a positive step.

B. Police Training

The Bush Administration has sought to address the investigative failings in Guatemala through the Harvard Program and other administration of justice assistance, and through the Justice Department's International Criminal Investigation Training and Assistance Program (ICITAP) for the police. However, as this report demonstrates, these programs have not yielded satisfactory results. As noted in Chapter I, Harvard ended its participation in Guatemala after determining that the military would not let investigations into political killings proceed. ICITAP's police training program continues, despite the Bush Administration's suspension of military aid.

If the sole criteria for determining the value of the ICITAP program were the need for improving police criminal investigations, this report would provide a strong argument in its favor. The program offers courses lasting from a few days to several months which are intended to teach police, judges, and prosecutors "to use physical evidence to corroborate witness and victim testimony rather than to rely solely on confessions..."[90] Yet ICITAP has very little to show for its five years of training of hundreds of Guatemalan police officers, as well as the donation of modern forensic equipment and laboratories.[91] As demonstrated in this report, the manner in which the Guatemalan police handle criminal investigations remains deeply

---

[90] U.S. Department of State, Bureau of Public Affairs, "Criminal Justice and Democracy in the Western Hemisphere," April 1989.

[91] ICITAP has also provided training to judges, prosecutors, and investigators with the office of the Human Rights Ombudsman. However, the bulk of training and assistance has been provided to the National Police.

flawed. Of greater concern is the fact that the police themselves carry out gross violations of human rights, including torture, murder and disappearances.

● *The governments of the United States and other countries should end all training or assistance to the Guatemalan police as long as its members continue to commit gross violations of human rights and until the force demonstrates the political will to conduct serious investigations of crimes, including those committed by members of the security forces and their agents.*

C. Other Assistance for Medicolegal Investigations

During our visit to Guatemala, Americas Watch and Physicians for Human Rights found a tremendous interest on the part of judges, doctors, firemen, and both governmental and non-governmental human rights workers for training in the application of scientific and medical procedures in death investigations.

● *Private organizations, such as the American Association for the Advancement of Science and the Inter–American Institute for Human Rights, and the ICITAP program should provide training to these professionals to improve their ability to conduct investigations of violations of human rights.*

● *International and U.S. forensic science associations, such as the International Forensic Society and the American Academy of Forensic Sciences, should also establish exchange programs that will enable Guatemalan forensic doctors to receive training abroad.*

D. The Medicolegal System

After more than 30 years of almost continuous military rule, Guatemala's medicolegal system remains archaic and hopelessly bureaucratic. Its forensic doctors are no more than cogs in a convoluted and largely ineffective judicial system -- a situation that many of the doctors themselves recognize and regret. While these doctors may want to be more active death investigators, antiquated laws and attitudes keep them isolated in their autopsy rooms.

● *The Guatemalan government should begin to upgrade its medicolegal system by adopting the standards set forth in the United*

Nations Model Autopsy Protocol and the Model Protocol for Disinterment and Analysis of Skeletal Remains (see Appendices C and D).

• *The Guatemalan government should revise its code of criminal procedure so as to allow forensic doctors prompt and regular access to crime scenes and to witness testimony.*

• *The Guatemalan government should increase the number of forensic doctors so they can adequately carry out their professional responsibilities.*

• *The Guatemalan government should upgrade morgue and laboratory facilities and provide forensic doctors with modern equipment.*

• *The president of the Supreme Court of Guatemala should turn over the new morgue facilities in Guatemala City, which have been in disuse for three years, to the forensic doctors employed by the judicial morgue.*

• *The Department of Medicine at the University of San Carlos in Guatemala City should include courses in forensic pathology, radiology, and odontology as a regular part of its curriculum.*

E. Exhumations and Guatemala's Disappeared

Guatemala's disappeared and those persons known to have been killed for political reasons should not be forgotten. Thousands of them now lie buried in unmarked graves. Many of the relatives of the disappeared want a full accounting of their missing family members. They want the remains of their loved ones exhumed and identified and given a proper burial. They want the individuals responsible for their deaths prosecuted. The exhumations at San Antonio Sinaché in December 1990 and January 1991 demonstrated the value of using scientific methods and procedures to exhume unmarked graves, to identify the remains, and to determine the cause and manner of death.

• *The Guatemalan government should ensure that those involved in exhumations have been trained in the scientific techniques and procedures used to disinter skeletal remains.*

● *The newly established Commission on the Disappeared should work with the relatives of the disappeared and their associations to collect ante–mortem data for the identification of the remains of the disappeared. Such data should include the physical characteristics of the disappeared person (sex, race, stature, handedness, age at death); all medical X–rays and dental records; photographs of the deceased; and physical descriptions of all injuries, especially fractures.*

● *Any medicolegal investigation of the disappeared should include an attempt to determine the victim's identity and the cause and manner of death.*

F. Investigations and Political Will

Guatemala's civilian authorities are ultimately responsible for ensuring that all violations of human rights are investigated in a fair, thorough, and prompt manner. And until they take this responsibility seriously, Guatemala will continue to be viewed as a country where the state and its agents can get away with murder.

● *The Guatemalan government should undertake serious investigations leading to prosecutions of such notorious crimes as the murder of Myrna Mack and the massacre of 13 peaceful protesters at Santiago Atitlán. The highest military and civilian authorities should publicly express support for the investigations and prosecutions and should make clear that those among their ranks who have committed abuses will be tried and punished.*

● *The government should carry out the arrest warrants issued by judges against civil patrollers suspected in the abduction and murder of Sebastián Velásquez Mejía, the murders of Manuel Perebal Morales and Juan Perebal Xirúm as well as the serious wounding of Diego Perebal León, all of them human rights monitors. Arrest warrants issued in January against the former civil patrol chief of San Antonio Sinaché for the murder of several villagers should also be executed. Once the suspects are detained, every effort should be made to be sure they receive independent, prompt, and fair trials. Extraordinary measures should be taken to guarantee the security of judges, witnesses, and human rights monitors involved in the cases.*

G. The Protection of Human Rights Monitors

The protection of human rights activists in Guatemala ought to be the foremost concern of all those who advocate respect for human rights and genuine democratic government in that country. Serious, prompt, and effective measures must be taken to halt the violence against the human rights community.

● *The highest military and civilian authorities should publicly declare that they recognize the legitimacy of the work of human rights monitors in Guatemala and acknowledge that their activities are protected by the Constitution of Guatemala.*

● *The military should cease all propaganda activities against human rights groups.*

● *The civilian and military authorities should order all government forces, including the civil patrols, to cease the campaign of violence and harassment against human rights activists. In addition, the authorities should make clear their intentions to prosecute and punish those responsible for persecution of human rights monitors.*

APPENDIX A

Forensic Investigative Report
Re: Myrna Elizabeth Mack Chang

FORENSIC INVESTIGATIVE REPORT

RE: MYRNA ELIZABETH MACK CHANG
DATE OF DEATH: 11 SEPTEMBER 1990

On 11 September 1990, Myrna Mack, a social scientist and co-founder of AVANCSO, was murdered near her office in Guatemala City, Guatemala. This review of the forensic evidence surrounding her death was undertaken at the request of Helen Mack, sister of the deceased, Americas Watch, Physicians for Human Rights and other interested individuals and organizations in Guatemala and the United States.

The following documents and materials were reviewed:

1. The autopsy report, including hand-written notes and body diagrams prepared at the time of the autopsy
2. Toxicology and serology report
3. Eighteen black and white crime scene photographs, 11.5 x 8.5 cm each, and a 25 x 20 cm enlargement of each photo
4. Ten black and white autopsy photographs, 11.5 x 8.5 cm each, and a 25 x 20 cm enlargement of each photo
5. One white blouse with pale blue edging, pale blue slacks and a white bra, worn by Myrna Mack at the time of her death
6. Background information prepared by AVANCSO related to the context and circumstances of the death of Myrna Mack
7. Court records released to Helen Mack

The following individuals with specific knowledge of the case were interviewed in Guatemala City in December, 1990:

1. Helen Mack
2 An official of the Department of Criminal Investigation (DIC) of the National Police
3. The forensic physician who performed the autopsy, Dr. Gilberto Sajche Sosa

In addition to the above, the scene photographs and autopsy photographs were presented to forensic pathologists and other forensic specialists attending a session at the American Academy of Forensic Sciences meeting in February 1991 devoted to the analysis of puzzling cases. The photographs and clothing were also examined by an independent forensic specialist.

Based upon the above review, I offer the following comments upon the investigation into the death of Myrna Mack:

1. THE AUTOPSY

The autopsy protocol, notes, diagrams and photographs permit an adequate review of the injuries sustained by Myrna, although not all of the stab wounds and cutting wounds are documented photographically. The wounds could all have been inflicted with a single weapon, but their appearance is relatively non-specific, and two weapons could have been used. There is nothing in the pattern of injuries to indicate whether one or more assailants were involved. This question will be discussed further below, in the consideration of the crime scene.

The characteristics of the injuries are most consistent with a single edged knife of medium size. There is no evidence of serration, although the upper wound on the left side of the neck has a somewhat ragged appearance.

The distribution of the wounds, including the several "defense" wounds of the arms and right hand, are clear evidence of a struggle. There are no "defense" wounds of the left hand, which grasped the length of plastic that is now missing or discarded. The wound of the right side of the body shows an apparent abrasion at the upper end of the wound that may be a hilt mark of the knife used in the assault. The larger dark mark below the wound may be another abrasion.

I do not detect any specific injuries to the body other than the stab wounds and cutting wounds. On the upper third of the anterior aspect of the left forearm there are several small marks and regions of discoloration noted in the photograph of the left arm. The enlargement of this photo suggests that these are patterned contusions and abrasions, but they may represent only areas of dried and smeared blood.

Finally, it is also noted that the right hand is visible in one photograph, and that it is enclosed within a clear plastic bag. It does not appear to have been fingerprinted. The left hand is not observed. There are conflicting versions about when the bags were removed and the hands printed. The hands were not, however, examined for trace evidence by either the police or the physician performing the postmortem examination.

2. THE CLOTHING

Myrna Mack's clothing was returned to Helen Mack without having been examined by forensic laboratory personnel, and was then washed and made available to Americas Watch. The opportunity to retrieve trace evidence that might have linked an assailant to this crime was thus lost by the failure of authorities to retain this evidence.

Examination of the tears in the blouse associated with the stab wounds of the body shows them to be of a similar type, consistent with one weapon, most likely with a single edged blade. The tears measure from 1.5 cm to 2.5 cm in length, with the majority measuring approximately 2.0 cm. Occasional puncture type tears and larger tears are noted. There are 4 tears on the upper left side of the blouse, one in the left breast pocket region, one on the upper right side, a 6.5 cm tear near the bottom right front, one in the left upper back, one in the left middle, and 4 in the lower back, and 3 on the left sleeve, for a total of 18. All of these are not associated with injuries to the body. There are 2 tears in the left bra cup and a single vertical tear at the left knee region of the slacks.

3. THE SCENE INVESTIGATION

There was a total failure to process the crime scene in an appropriate manner, and to retain evidence necessary for the evaluation of this case.

As is clearly evident from the pattern of blood splatter and pooling, the assault was marked by an extensive struggle. Analysis of the blood splatter pattern does not provide additional information regarding the number of assailants. It is likely, however, that significant traces of blood would have been deposited on the assailant's (s') clothing.

The significance of the bloody shoeprints was dismissed, claiming that they were the shoeprints of curious bystanders or of the voluntary firemen at the scene. Indeed, in one photograph a small amount of dark stain, consistent with blood, is noted on the left shoe heel of a fireman placing a sheet over the body of Myrna Mack. There is no indication of the chronology of the photographs, but it is significant that in all of the photos the same shoeprints are seen. This, despite the fact that there is evidence of continued movement of personnel with the body being photographed uncovered, partially covered by a stretcher, and covered by a sheet. If the prints were those of the firemen, then there should have been more shoeprints in the later photos rather than the same number throughout the activity at the scene. This indicates that the prints were present prior to the scene being disturbed by the firemen and the police.

The prints are not those of ordinary civilian shoes, but are characteristic of some type of boot. Analysis of these prints at the scene and in the laboratory according to usual forensic standards would have provided evidence as to shoe size, number of different shoe prints, the style of the shoe, and perhaps its manufacturer. This evidence is now lost.

Grasped in Mack's left hand is a length of twisted white plastic material, consistent with a ligature. It remains unclear, because of conflicting stories, whether this evidence was lost or discarded as "unimportant." It is unlikely that it is the handle of a plastic bag stolen in a robbery attempt. If this was a robbery, there would have been no reason for such a violent struggle to retain possession of a shopping bag. If the bag had been literally "ripped off", the handle portion remaining in Myrna's hand should have been stretched and showed frayed ends. In fact, the plastic is moderately twisted, appears too long to be a bag handle, and is thus more likely to be a ligature. This length of plastic should have been evaluated for fingerprints, and retained for a possible match to its corresponding portion, which might have remained in the custody of the assailant(s).

4. CONCLUSIONS

There were probably two assailants - one wielding a knife, and the other attempting to Choke or bind their victim. Those involved were relatively inexperienced. It is improbable that professionals would allow themselves to be caught in a struggle that could attract considerable attention and provide so much potentially incriminating evidence. Within the context of the political situation in Guatemala, the crime probably reflects a failed attempt to kidnap Myrna Mack, rather than simply kill her, which could have been done easily in the usual manner with a gun.

The inadequacies of the forensic aspects of this death investigation demonstrate a failure to follow accepted methods of obtaining and securing evidence. It is equally the case that there is an obvious lack of willingness to pursue appropriate investigative leads to track down Myrna Mack's assailants - i.e., locate the individuals who had her under surveillance.

Respectfully submitted,

Robert H. Kirschner, M.D.
Deputy Chief Medical Examiner, Cook County, Illinois
Clinical Associate, Department of Pathology
University of Chicago

15 May, 1991

APPENDIX B

HUMAN SKELETAL REMAINS EXHUMED FROM SAN ANTONIO DE SINACHE, GUATEMALA ON JANUARY 9, 1991

91-002GUA: HUMAN SKELETAL REMAINS EXHUMED FROM SAN ANTONIO DE SINACHE, GUATEMALA ON JANUARY 9, 1991 (Case Series # SAS 2)

DATE OF EXAMINATION: January 10, 1991

PLACE OF EXAMINATION: Morgue, National Hospital, Santa Cruz de Quiché, Guatemala.

CASE SUMMARY

The skeleton is that of a young adult American Indian male. Based on the condition of the skeleton, death occurred between 4 and 9 years prior to exhumation. Death was caused by two gunshot wounds to the head.

The grave was unmarked. No coffin or gravegoods except clothing were found with the victim.

INVENTORY

The skeleton was complete except for eight small bones of the hands (4 carpals, 1 proximal phalanx, 2 intermediate phalanges and 1 terminal phalanx) which were not recovered during exhumation. In the spinal skeleton, this individual exhibited a 6th lumbar vertebra -- a variation that occurs in about 5% to 10% of adults. The bones recovered represent 96.0% of a complete skeleton.

The following items of clothing were removed from the skeleton:

1. Wide brimmed straw hat.
2. Long-sleeved, light brown with a flowered pattern, front-buttoned shirt with collar.
3. An undershirt of burgundy color, v-bottom front with knit material on upper arm and over breast on each shoulder. No label.
4. Black leather belt. 4 cm. wide with metal buckle with insignia of a spurred boot.
5. Dark blue zippered trousers.

6. Underpants consist of a bathing trunks, multicolor pattern, zippered front.
7. Rubber–tire sandals, 21 cm long, 10 cm wide.

When exhumed, a blindfold in the form of a knotted handkerchief was still in place on the skull.

SEX: MALE

Sexual diagnosis is based on morphological traits of the pelvis which are distinctly masculine. These include the strongly–arched iliac crest, narrow sciatic notch, acute subpubic angle and triangulate pubis. The cranium also exhibited strong masculine traits, including a robust supra–orbital torus, large mastoid processes and strongly–developed nuchal musculature ridges.

RACE: MONGOLOID (American Indian)

The cranial vault is relatively wide. Sutural serration is simple. The facial skeleton is broad, with strong, angular and anteriorly projecting malars. The nasal bridge is wide and low, the nasal aperture relatively broad with fasciculate inferior nasal margins. Facial profile is orthognathous. Palate is very broad and shallow and the maxillary and mandibular incisors shovel–shaped. This configuration of cranial traits are typically mongoloid.

AGE AT DEATH: (20–24 years)

The basilar suture is closed. Cranial vault sutures are open. Dentition is fully adult. Long bone epiphyses are closed. The medial clavicular epiphysis shows minimal (Stage 1) fusion. The first sacral segment is still open. The vertebral centra are incompletely fused from C4 to L1.

Degenerative age changes in the form of osteoarthritic lipping of the major joints or vertebral osteophytosis are absent. Periodontal disease and dental attrition is slight.

Pubic symphysial morphology is assessed using the McKern–Stewart system (Table 1).

TABLE 1

===
PUBIC SYMPHYSIAL AGE ESTIMATE
===

CASE: 91002GUA (SAS-2)

COMPONENT				
I Dorsal	3.0	SEX:	Male
II Ventral	1.5	AGE:	21.8 years
III Rim	1.5	SEest:	1.0 years
		MINIMUM:	19.8 years
Symphysial Score	6.0	MAXIMUM:	23.8 years

Ref: McKern & Stewart '57, Gilbert & McKern '73, Snow '83

The total symphysial score of 6.5 corresponds to an age estimate of 21.8 years with a 95% confidence range of about 20–24 years and is thus consistent with the more general findings discussed above.

ANTEMORTEM STATURE: 156–169 cm.

Antemortem stature is estimated from the combined maximum lengths of the femur and tibia, using the Trotter–Glesser equations for Mongoloid males (Table 2). The midpoint estimate is 163.0 which falls within a 95% probability range of about 156–169 cm.

TABLE 2

===

ANTEMORTEM STATURE PREDICTED FROM
LONG BONE LENGTHS

===

CASE 91002GUA, SAS2 SEX: Male   RACE: Mongoloid
AGE: 21 yrs

LONG BONE LENGTHS
ESTIMATED FROM: Femur + Tibia   759 mm

Bone Length	(mm)		Cm.	In.
1. Femur	421	STATURE:	163.0	64.2
2. Tibia	338	SEest:	3.2	1.3
	------	−2SEest:	156.5	61.6
TOTAL	759	+2SEest:	169.4	66.7
	AGE CORRECTION:		0.0	0.0

Ref: Trotter '70

HANDEDNESS: Right-handed.
Beveling of the scapular posterior glenoid rim is more pronounced on the right. The right upper extremity bones exceed the left in length and their muscular attachments are more pronounced. These findings indicate that the subject was right-handed.

DENTITION
Complete with no restorations

ANTEMORTEM PATHOLOGIES
No signs of antemortem disease, anomalies or trauma were present.

PERIMORTEM TRAUMA
Perimortem trauma is present as two through-and-through small-caliber gunshot wounds of the head. The inwardly-beveled entrance wounds are located in the posterior left parietal. The most medial of these is situated 39 mm from the from the midline, 20 mm above the lambdoid suture: it is circular, measuring 7mm in diameter. The second entrance wound is located 23 mm lateral and slightly inferior to the first. It is 60 mm from the midline and 26 mm superior to the lambdoid suture. Like the first, it is inwardly beveled, circular and measures 7 mm diameter.

The exit wounds are located on the right lateral cranial vault. The most anterior of these is in the frontal bone, immediately anterior to the fronto-sphenoid suture, 18 mm posterior to the left superior orbital margin and 69 mm anterior-superior to the right external auditory meatus: it is outwardly beveled, ovoid, and measures 7 mm by 11 mm on the external cranial surface. The posterior-most of the exit wounds is situated in the greater wing of the sphenoid, just in front of the anterior border of the temporal bone. It is 27 mm posterior to the left lateral orbital margin and 47 mm anterior-superior to the right external auditory meatus: it is outwardly beveled, ovoid and measures 7 mm by 12 mm in its axial diameters.

A deformed .22 caliber bullet was found by the skull during exhumation.

TIME OF DEATH:

No datable artifacts were recovered from the grave. Based on the general condition of the skeleton, I would estimate death as occurring about 3 to 7 years prior to disinterment.

CAUSE OF DEATH

Death was caused by two small-caliber gunshot wounds entering the left-posterior cranial vault, travelling transversely and to the right to exit in the right anterior cranial vault. The close spacing of the two exit wounds and their nearly parallel trajectories suggest that the victim was immobile at the time the shots were fired. It is thus possible that he was lying on the ground in a supine position when he was shot. A blindfold was still in place on the skull when the remains were found.

ADDITIONAL REMARKS

It is important to note that this case and that of SAS-3 have certain significant features in common. Both were found in unmarked graves situated within a few meters of each other. Both crania were found with blindfolds still in place and both died from two closely-spaced, small-caliber (probably .22 caliber long rimfire bullets) fired into the right side of the head. These findings suggest a common *modus operandi* and, perhaps, a single perpetrator.

Clyde Collins Snow, Ph.D.

February 28, 1991

APPENDICES C AND D

Minnesota Protocol I--Model Autopsy Protocol
And
Minnesota Protocol II--Model Protocol for Disinterment and Analysis of Skeletal Remains

Appendices C and D are part of the *Manual on the Effective Prevention and Investigation of Extra-Legal, Arbitrary and Summary Executions*, published by the United Nations in 1991. The purpose of the manual is to aid judges, lawyers, forensic specialists, law enforcement personnel, advocates of human rights, and relatives of human rights abuses in the investigation of the following deaths: (a) political assassinations; (b) deaths resulting from torture or ill-treatment in prison or detention; (c) death resulting from enforced "disappearances"; (d) deaths resulting from the excessive use of force by law enforcement personnel; (e) executions without due process; and (f) acts of genocide. For information on how to obtain a copy of the manual in English, Spanish, or other languages, please telephone or write to the United Nations, Sales Section, New York, NY 10017 (Telephone: 212/963-8302).

IV. MODEL AUTOPSY PROTOCOL

A. Introduction

Difficult or sensitive cases should ideally be the responsibility of an objective, experienced, well-equipped and well-trained prosector (the person performing the autopsy and preparing the written report) who is separate from any potentially involved political organization or entity. Unfortunately, this ideal is often unattainable. This proposed model autopsy protocol includes a comprehensive checklist of the steps in a basic forensic postmortem examination that should be followed to the extent possible given the resources available. Use of this autopsy protocol will permit early and final resolution of potentially controversial cases and will thwart the speculation and innuendo that are fueled by unanswered, partially answered or poorly answered questions in the investigation of an apparently suspicious death.

This model autopsy protocol is intended to have several applications and may be of value to the following categories of individuals:

(a) Experienced forensic pathologists may follow this model autopsy protocol to ensure a systematic examination and to facilitate meaningful positive or negative criticism by later observers. While trained pathologists may justifiably abridge certain aspects of the postmortem examination or written descriptions of their findings in routine cases, abridged examinations or reports are never appropriate in potentially controversial cases. Rather, a systematic and comprehensive examination and report are required to prevent the omission or loss of important details;

(b) General pathologists or other physicians who have not been trained in forensic pathology but are familiar with basic postmortem examination techniques may supplement their customary autopsy procedures with this model autopsy protocol. It may also alert them to situations in which they should seek consultation, as written material cannot replace the knowledge gained through experience;

(c) Independent consultants whose expertise has been requested in observing, performing or reviewing an autopsy may cite this model autopsy protocol and its proposed minimum criteria as a basis for their actions or opinions;

(d) Governmental authorities, international political organizations, law enforcement agencies, families or friends of decedents, or representatives of potential defendants charged with responsibility for a death may use this model autopsy protocol to establish appropriate procedures for the postmortem examination prior to its performance;

(e) Historians, journalists, attorneys, judges, other physicians and representatives of the public may also use this model autopsy protocol as a benchmark for evaluating an autopsy and its findings;

(f) Governments or individuals who are attempting either to establish or upgrade their medicolegal system for investigating deaths may use this model autopsy protocol as a guideline, representing the procedures and goals to be incorporated into an ideal medicolegal system.

While performing any medicolegal death investigation, the prosector should collect information that will establish the identity of the deceased, the time and place of death, the cause of death, and the manner or mode of death (homicide, suicide, accident or natural).

It is of the utmost importance that an autopsy performed following a controversial death be thorough in scope. The documentation and recording of the autopsy findings should be equally thorough so as to permit meaningful use of the autopsy results (see annex II, below). It is important to have as few omissions or discrepancies as possible, as proponents of different interpretations of a case may take advantage of any perceived shortcomings in the investigation. An autopsy performed in a controversial death should meet certain minimum criteria if the autopsy report is to be proffered as meaningful or conclusive by the prosector, the autopsy's sponsoring agency or governmental unit, or anyone else attempting to make use of such an autopsy's findings or conclusions.

This model autopsy protocol is designed to be used in diverse situations. Resources such as autopsy rooms, X-ray equipment or adequately trained personnel are not available everywhere. Forensic pathologists must operate under widely divergent political systems. In addition, social and religious customs vary widely throughout the world; an autopsy is an expected and routine procedure in some areas, while it is abhorred in others. A prosector, therefore, may not always be able to follow all of the steps in this protocol when performing autopsies. Variation from this protocol may be inevitable or even preferable in some cases. It is suggested, however, that any major deviations, with the supporting reasons, should be noted.

It is important that the body should be made available to the prosector for a minimum of 12 hours in order to assure an adequate and unhurried examination. Unrealistic limits or conditions are occasionally placed upon the prosector with respect to the length of time permitted for the examination or the circumstances under which an examination is allowed. When conditions are imposed, the prosector should be able to refuse to perform a compromised examination and should prepare a report explaining this position. Such a refusal should not be interpreted as indicating that an examination was unnecessary or inappropriate. If the prosector decides to proceed with the examination notwithstanding difficult conditions or circumstances, he or she should include in the autopsy report an explanation of the limitations or impediments.

Certain steps in this model autopsy protocol have been emphasized by the use of **boldface type**. These represent the most essential elements of the protocol.

B. Proposed model autopsy protocol

1. Scene investigation

The prosector(s) and medical investigators should have the right of access to the scene where the body is found. **The medical personnel should be notified immediately to assure that no alteration of the body has occurred. If access to the scene was denied, if the body was altered or if information was withheld, this should be stated in the prosector's report.**

A system for co-ordination between the medical and non-medical investigators (e.g. law enforcement agencies) should be established. This should address such issues as how the prosector will be notified and who will be in charge of the scene. Obtaining certain types of evidence is often the role of the non-medical investigators, but the medical investigators who have access to the body at the scene of death should perform the following steps:

(a) **Photograph the body as it is found** and after it has been moved;

(b) Record the body position and condition, including body **warmth** or

(c)   Protect the deceased's hands, e.g. with paper bags;

(d)   Note the ambient temperature. In cases where the time of death is an issue, rectal temperature should be recorded and any insects present should be collected for forensic entomological study. Which procedure is applicable will depend on the length of the apparent postmortem interval;

(e)   Examine the scene for blood, as this may be useful in identifying suspects;

(f)   Record the identities of all persons at the scene;

(g)   Obtain information from scene witnesses, including those who last saw the decedent alive, and when, where and under what circumstances. Interview any emergency medical personnel who may have had contact with the body;

(h)   Obtain identification of the body and other pertinent information from friends or relatives. Obtain the deceased's medical history from his or her physician(s) and hospital charts, including any previous surgery, alcohol or drug use, suicide attempts and habits;

(i)   Place the body in a body pouch or its equivalent. Save this pouch after the body has been removed from it;

(j)   Store the body in a secure refrigerated location so that tampering with the body and its evidence cannot occur;

(k)   Make sure that projectiles, guns, knives and other weapons are available for examination by the responsible medical personnel;

(l)   If the decedent was hospitalized prior to death, obtain admission or blood specimens and any X-rays, and review and summarize hospital records;

(m)   Before beginning the autopsy, become familiar with the types of torture or violence that are prevalent in that country or locale (see annex III).

2. Autopsy

The following Protocol should be followed during the autopsy:

(a)   Record the date, starting and finishing times, and place of the autopsy (a complex autopsy may take as long as an entire working day);

(b)   Record the name(s) of the prosector(s), the participating assistant(s), and all other persons present during the autopsy, including the medical and/or scientific degrees and professional, political or administrative affiliations(s) of each. Each person's role in the autopsy should be indicated, and one person should be designated as the principal prosector who will have the authority to direct the performance of the autopsy. Observers and other team members are subject to direction by, and should not interfere with, the principal prosector. The time(s) during the autopsy when each person is present should be included. The use of a "sign-in" sheet is recommended;

(c)   Adequate photographs are crucial for thorough documentation of autopsy findings:

(i)   Photographs should be in colour (transparency or negative/
      print), in focus, adequately illuminated, and taken by a
      professional or good quality camera. Each photograph should
      contain a ruled reference scale, an identifying case name or
      number, and a sample of standard grey. A description of the
      camera (including the lens "f-number" and focal length), film
      and the lighting system must be included in the autopsy report.
      If more than one camera is utilized, the identifying informa-
      tion should be recorded for each. Photographs should also
      include information indicating which camera took each picture,
      if more than one camera is used. The identity of the person
      taking the photographs should be recorded;

(ii) Serial photographs reflecting the course of the external
      examination must be included. Photograph the body prior to and
      following undressing, washing or cleaning and shaving;

(iii) Supplement close-up photographs with distant and/or immediate
      range photographs to permit orientation and identification of
      the close-up photographs;

(iv) Photographs should be comprehensive in scope and must confirm
      the presence of all demonstrable signs of injury or disease
      commented upon in the autopsy report;

(v)   Identifying facial features should be portrayed (after washing
      or cleaning the body), with photographs of a full frontal
      aspect of the face, and right and left profiles of the face
      with hair in normal position and with hair retracted, if
      necessary, to reveal the ears;

(d) **Radiograph the body** before it is removed from its pouch or
wrappings. X-rays should be repeated both before and after undressing the
body. Fluoroscopy may also be performed. **Photograph all X-ray films;**

(i)   **Obtain dental X-rays**, even if identification has been
      established in other ways;

(ii) **Document any skeletal system injury by X-ray.** Skeletal X-rays
      may also record anatomic defects or surgical procedures. Check
      especially for fractures of the fingers, toes and other bones
      in the hands and feet. Skeletal X-rays may also aid in the
      identification of the deceased, by detecting identifying
      characteristics, estimating age and height, and determining
      sex and race. Frontal sinus films should also be taken, as
      these can be particularly useful for identification purposes;

(iii) Take X-rays in gunshot cases to aid in locating the
      projectile(s). Recover, photograph and save any projectile or
      major projectile fragment that is seen on an X-ray. Other
      radio-opaque objects **(pacemakers, artificial joints or valves,
      knife fragments etc.)** documented with X-rays should also be
      removed, photographed and saved;

(iv) Skeletal X-rays are essential in children **to assist in deter-
      mining age and developmental status;**

(e) Before the clothing is removed, examine the body and the clothing. Photograph the clothed body. Record any jewellery present;

(f) The clothing should be carefully removed over a clean sheet or body pouch. Let the clothing dry if it is bloody or wet. Describe the clothing that is removed and label it in a permanent fashion. Either place the clothes in the custody of a responsible person or keep them, as they may be useful as evidence or for identification;

(g) The external examination, focusing on a search for external evidence of injury is, in most cases, the most important portion of the autopsy;

    (i) Photograph all surfaces - 100 per cent of the body area. Take good quality, well-focused, colour photographs with adequate illumination;

    (ii) Describe and document the means used to make the identification. Examine the body and record the deceased's apparent age, length, weight, sex, head hair style and length, nutritional status, muscular development and colour of skin, eyes and hair (head, facial and body);

    (iii) In children, measure also the head circumference, crown-rump length and crown-heel length;

    (iv) Record the degree, location and fixation of rigor and livor mortis;

    (v) Note body warmth or coolness and state of preservation; note any decomposition changes, such as skin slippage. Evaluate the general condition of the body and note adipocere formation, maggots, eggs or anything else that suggests the time or place of death;

    (vi) With all injuries, record the size, shape, pattern, location (related to obvious anatomic landmarks), colour, course, direction, depth and structure involved. Attempt to distinguish injuries resulting from therapeutic measures from those unrelated to medical treatment. In the description of projectile wounds, note the presence or absence of soot, gunpowder, or singeing. If gunshot residue is present, document it photographically and save it for analysis. Attempt to determine whether the gunshot wound is an entry or exit wound. If an entry wound is present and no exit wound is seen, the projectile must be found and saved or accounted for. Excise wound tract tissue samples for microscopic examination. Tape together the edges of knife wounds to assess the blade size and characteristics;

    (vii) Photograph all injuries, taking two colour pictures of each, labelled with the autopsy identification number on a scale that is oriented parallel or perpendicular to the injury. Shave hair where necessary to clarify an injury, and take photographs before and after shaving. Save all hair removed from the site of the injury. Take photographs before and after washing the site of any injury. Wash the body only after any blood or material that may have come from an assailant has been collected and saved;

(viii)   Examine the skin. Note and photograph any scars, areas of
         keloid formation, tattoos, prominent moles, areas of increased
         or decreased pigmentation, and anything distinctive or unique
         such as birthmarks. Note any bruises and incise them for
         delineation of their extent. Excise them for microscopic exam-
         ination. The head and genital area should be checked with
         special care. Note any injection sites or puncture wounds
         and excise them to use for toxicological evaluation. Note any
         abrasions and excise them; microscopic sections may be useful
         for attempting to date the time of injury. Note any bite
         marks; these should be photographed to record the dental
         pattern, swabbed for saliva testing (before the body is washed)
         and excised for microscopic examination. Bite marks should also
         be analysed by a forensic odontologist, if possible. Note any
         burn marks and attempt to determine the cause (burning rubber,
         a cigarette, electricity, a blowtorch, acid, hot oil etc.).
         Excise any suspicious areas for microscopic examination, as it
         may be possible to distinguish microscopically between burns
         caused by electricity and those caused by heat;

(ix)   Identify and label any foreign object that is recovered,
         including its relation to specific injuries. Do not scratch
         the sides or tip of any projectiles. Photograph each projec-
         tile and large projectile fragment with an identifying label,
         and then place each in a sealed, padded and labelled container
         in order to maintain the chain of custody;

(x)   Collect a blood specimen of at least 50 cc from a subclavian
         or femoral vessel;

(xi)   Examine the head and external scalp, bearing in mind that
         injuries may be hidden by the hair. Shave hair where necessary.
         Check for fleas and lice, as these may indicate unsanitary con-
         ditions prior to death. Note any alopecia as this may be caused
         by malnutrition, heavy metals (e.g. thallium), drugs or trac-
         tion. Pull, do not cut, 20 representative head hairs and save
         them, as hair may also be useful for detecting some drugs and
         poisons;

(xii)   Examine the teeth and note their condition. Record any that
         are absent, loose or damaged, and record all dental work
         (restorations, fillings etc.), using a dental identification
         system to identify each tooth. Check the gums for periodontal
         disease. Photograph dentures, if any, and save them if the
         decedent's identity is unknown. Remove the mandible and
         maxilla if necessary for identification. Check the inside of
         the mouth and note any evidence of trauma, injection sites,
         needle marks or biting of the lips, cheeks or tongue. Note
         any articles or substances in the mouth. In cases of suspected
         sexual assault, save oral fluid or get a swab for spermatozoa
         and acid phosphatase evaluation. (Swabs taken at the tooth-gum
         junction and samples from between the teeth provide the best
         specimens for identifying spermatozoa.) Also take swabs from
         the oral cavity for seminal fluid typing. Dry the swabs quickly
         with cool, blown air if possible, and preserve them in clean
         plain paper envelopes. If rigor mortis prevents an adequate
         examination, the masseter muscles may be cut to permit better
         exposure;

(xiii) Examine the face and note if it is cyanotic or if petechiae are present;

    a. Examine the eyes and view the conjunctiva of both the globes and the eyelids. Note any petechiae in the upper or lower eyelids. Note any scleral icterus. Save contact lenses, if any are present. Collect at least 1 ml of vitreous humor from each eye;

    b. Examine the nose and ears and note any evidence of trauma, haemorrhage or other abnormalities. Examine the tympanic membranes;

(xiv) Examine the neck externally on all aspects and note any contusions, abrasions or petechiae. Describe and document injury patterns to differentiate manual, ligature and hanging strangulation. Examine the neck at the conclusion of the autopsy, when the blood has drained out of the area and the tissues are dry;

(xv) Examine all surfaces of the extremities: arms, forearms, wrists, hands, legs and feet, and note any "defence" wounds. Dissect and describe any injuries. Note any bruises about the wrists or ankles that may suggest restraints such as hand-cuffs or suspension. Examine the medial and lateral surfaces of the fingers, the anterior forearms and the backs of the knees for bruises;

(xvi) Note any broken or missing fingernails. Note any gunpowder residue on the hands, document photographically and save it for analysis. Take fingerprints in all cases. If the decedent's identity is unknown and fingerprints cannot be obtained, remove the "glove" of the skin, if present. Save the fingers if no other means of obtaining fingerprints is possible. Save finger-nail clippings and any under-nail tissue (nail scrapings). Examine the fingernail and toenail beds for evidence of objects having been pushed beneath the nails. Nails can be removed by dissecting the lateral margins and proximal base, and then the undersurface of the nails can be inspected. If this is done, the hands must be photographed before and after the nails are removed. Carefully examine the soles of the feet, noting any evidence of beating. Incise the soles to delineate the extent of any injuries. Examine the palms and knees, looking especially for glass shards or lacerations;

(xvii) Examine the external genitalia and note the presence of any foreign material or semen. Note the size, location and number of any abrasions or contusions. Note any injury to the inner thighs or peri-anal area. Look for peri-anal burns;

(xviii) In cases of suspected sexual assault, examine all potentially involved orifices. A speculum should be used to examine the vaginal walls. Collect foreign hair by combing the pubic hair. Pull and save at least 20 of the deceased's own pubic hairs, including roots. Aspirate fluid from the vagina and/or rectum for acid phosphatase, blood group and spermatozoa evaluation. Take swabs from the same areas for seminal fluid typing. Dry the swabs quickly with cool, blown air if possible, and preserve them in clean plain paper envelopes;

(xix) The length of the back, the buttocks and extremities including
wrists and ankles must be systematically incised to look for
deep injuries. The shoulders, elbows, hips and knee joints
must also be incised to look for ligamentous injury;

(h) The internal examination for internal evidence of injury should
clarify and augment the external examination;

(i) Be systematic in the internal examination. **Perform the examination either by body regions or by systems, including the
cardiovascular, respiratory, biliary, gastrointestinal,
reticuloendothelial, genitourinary, endocrine, musculoskeletal,
and central nervous systems.** Record the weight, size, shape,
colour and consistency of each organ, and note any neoplasia,
inflammation, anomalies, haemorrhage, ischemia, infarcts,
surgical procedures or injuries. Take sections of normal and
any abnormal areas of each organ for microscopic examination.
**Take samples of any fractured bones for radiographic and
microscopic estimation of the age of the fracture;**

(ii) **Examine the chest.** Note any abnormalities of the breasts.
Record any rib fractures, noting whether cardiopulmonary
resuscitation was attempted. Before opening, check for
pneumothoraces. Record the thickness of subcutaneous fat.
Immediately after opening the chest, evaluate the pleural
cavities and the pericardial sac for the presence of blood or
other fluid, and describe and quantify any fluid present. Save
any fluid present until foreign objects are accounted for.
Note the presence of air embolism, characterized by frothy
blood within the right atrium and right ventricle. **Trace any
injuries before removing the organs.** If blood is not
available at other sites, collect a sample directly from the
heart. **Examine the heart,** noting degree and location of
coronary artery disease or other abnormalities. **Examine the
lungs,** noting any abnormalities;

(iii) **Examine the abdomen** and record the amount of subcutaneous
fat. Retain 50 grams of adipose tissue for toxicological
evaluation. Note the interrelationships of the organs. **Trace
any injuries before removing the organs.** Note any fluid or
blood present in the peritoneal cavity, and save it until
foreign objects are accounted for. **Save all urine** and bile
for toxicologic examination;

(iv) Remove, examine and record the quantitative information on the
liver, spleen, pancreas, kidneys and adrenal glands. Save at
least 150 grams each of kidney and liver **for toxicological**
evaluation. Remove the gastrointestinal tract and examine the
contents. Note any food present and its degree of digestion.
Save the contents of the stomach. If a more detailed toxicological evaluation is desired, the contents of other regions of
the gastrointestinal tract may be saved. **Examine the rectum
and anus** for burns, lacerations or other injuries. Locate and
retain any foreign bodies present. **Examine the aorta, inferior
vena cava and iliac vessels;**

(v)   Examine the organs in the pelvis, including ovaries, fallopian tubes, uterus, vagina, testes, prostate gland, seminal vesicles, urethra and urinary bladder. **Trace any injuries before removing the organs.** Remove these organs carefully so as not to injure them artifactually. Note any evidence of previous or current pregnancy, miscarriage or delivery. Save any foreign objects within the cervix, uterus, vagina, urethra or rectum;

(vi)   **Palpate the head** and examine the external and internal surfaces of the scalp, noting any trauma or haemorrhage. **Note any skull fractures.** Remove the calvarium carefully and note epidural and subdural haematomas. Quantify, date and save any haematomas that are present. Remove the dura to examine the internal surface of the skull for fractures. **Remove the brain** and note any abnormalities. **Dissect and describe any injuries.** Cerebral cortical atrophy, whether focal or generalized, should be specifically commented upon;

(vii)   Evaluate the cerebral vessels. Save at least 150 grams of cerebral tissue for toxicological evaluation. Submerge the brain in fixative prior to examination, if this is indicated;

(viii) **Examine the neck after the heart and brain have been removed and the neck vessels have been drained. Remove the neck organs,** taking care not to fracture the hyoid bone. **Dissect and describe any injuries.** Check the mucosa of the larynx, pyriform sinuses and esophagus, and note any petechiae, edema or burns caused by corrosive substances. Note any articles or substances within the lumina of these structures. Examine the thyroid gland. Separate and examine the parathyroid glands, if they are readily identifiable;

(ix)   Dissect the neck muscles, noting any haemorrhage. Remove all organs, including the tongue. Dissect the muscles from the bones and note any fractures of the hyoid bone or thyroid or cricoid cartilages;

(x)   **Examine the cervical, thoracic and lumbar spine.** Examine the vertebrae from their anterior aspects and note any fractures, dislocations, compressions or haemorrhages. Examine the vertebral bodies. Cerebrospinal fluid may be obtained if additional toxicological evaluation is indicated;

(xi)   **In cases in which spinal injury is suspected, dissect and describe the spinal cord.** Examine the cervical spine anteriorly and note any haemorrhage in the paravertebral muscles. The posterior approach is best for evaluating high cervical injuries. Open the spinal canal and remove the spinal cord. Make transverse sections every 0.5 cm and note any abnormalities;

(i) After the autopsy has been completed, **record which specimens have been saved.** Label all specimens with the name of the deceased, the autopsy identification number, the date and time of collection, the name of the prosector and the contents. **Carefully preserve all evidence and record the chain of custody with appropriate release forms;**

(i) Perform appropriate toxicologic tests and retain portions of the tested samples to permit retesting;

    a. Tissues: 150 grams of liver and kidney should be saved routinely. Brain, hair and adipose tissue may be saved for additional studies in cases where drugs, poisons or other toxic substances are suspected;

    b. Fluids: 50 cc (if possible) of blood (spin and save serum in all or some of the tubes), all available urine, vitreous humor and stomach contents should be saved routinely. Bile, regional gastrointestinal tract contents and cerebrospinal fluid should be saved in cases where drugs, poisons or toxic substances are suspected. Oral, vaginal and rectal fluid should be saved in cases of suspected sexual assault;

(ii) **Representative samples of all major organs, including areas of normal and any abnormal tissue, should be processed histologically and stained with hematoxylin and eosin (and other stains as indicated). The slides, wet tissue and paraffin blocks should be kept indefinitely;**

(iii) **Evidence that must be saved includes:**

    a. All foreign objects, including projectiles, projectile fragments, pellets, knives and fibres. **Projectiles must be subjected to ballistic analysis;**

    b. All clothes and personal effects of the deceased, worn by or in the possession of the deceased at the time of death;

    c. Fingernails and under nail scrapings;

    d. Hair, foreign and pubic, in cases of suspected sexual assault;

    e. Head hair, in cases where the place of death or location of the body prior to its discovery may be an issue;

(j) After the autopsy, all unretained organs should be replaced in the body, and the body should be well embalmed to facilitate a second autopsy in case one is desired at some future point;

(k) The written autopsy report should address those items that are emphasized in boldface type in the protocol. At the end of the autopsy report should be a summary of the findings and the cause of death. This should include the prosector's comments attributing any injuries to external trauma, therapeutic efforts, postmortem change, or other causes. A full report should be given to the appropriate authorities and to the deceased's family.

V. MODEL PROTOCOL FOR DISINTERMENT AND ANALYSIS OF SKELETAL REMAINS

A. Introduction

This proposed model protocol for the disinterment and analysis of skeletal remains includes a comprehensive checklist of the steps in a basic forensic examination. The objectives of an anthropological investigation are the same as those of a medicolegal investigation of a recently deceased person. The anthropologist must collect information that will establish the identity of the deceased, the time and place of death, the cause of death and the manner or mode of death (homicide, suicide, accident or natural). The approach of the anthropologist differs, however, because of the nature of the material to be examined. Typically, a prosector is required to examine a body, whereas an anthropologist is required to examine a skeleton. The prosector focuses on information obtained from soft tissues, whereas the anthropologist focuses on information from hard tissues. Since decomposition is a continuous process, the work of both specialists can overlap. An anthropologist may examine a fresh body when bone is exposed or when bone trauma is a factor. An experienced prosector may be required when mummified tissues are present. In some circumstances, use of both this protocol and the model autopsy protocol may be necessary to yield the maximum information. The degree of decomposition of the body will dictate the type of investigation and, therefore, the protocol(s) to be followed.

The questions addressed by the anthropologist differ from those pursued in a typical autopsy. The anthropological investigation invests more time and attention to basic questions such as the following:

(a) Are the remains human?

(b) Do they represent a single individual or several?

(c) What was the decedent's sex, race, stature, body weight, handedness and physique?

(d) Are there any skeletal traits or anomalies that could serve to positively identify the decedent?

The time, cause and manner of death are also addressed by the anthropologist, but the margin of error is usually greater than that which can be achieved by an autopsy shortly after death.

This model protocol may be of use in many diverse situations. Its application may be affected, however, by poor conditions, inadequate financial resources or lack of time. Variation from the protocol may be inevitable or even preferable in some cases. It is suggested, however, that any major deviations, with the supporting reasons, should be noted in the final report.

B. Proposed model skeletal analysis protocol

1. Scene investigation

A burial recovery should be handled with the same exacting care given to a crime-scene search. Efforts should be co-ordinated between the principal investigator and the consulting physical anthropologist or archaeologist. Human remains are frequently exhumed by law enforcement officers or cemetery workers unskilled in the techniques of forensic anthropology. Valuable information may be lost in this manner and false information is sometimes generated. Disinterment by untrained persons should be prohibited. The consulting anthropologist should be present to conduct or supervise the disinterment. Specific problems and procedures accompany the excavation of each type of burial. The amount of information obtained from the excavation depends on knowledge of the burial situation and judgement based on experience. The final report should include a rationale for the excavation procedure.

The following procedure should be followed during disinterment:

(a) Record the date, location, starting and finishing times of the disinterment, and the names of all workers;

(b) Record the information in narrative form, supplemented by sketches and photographs;

(c) Photograph the work area from the same perspective before work begins and after it ends every day to document any disturbance not related to the official procedure;

(d) In some cases, it is necessary to first locate the grave within a given area. There are numerous methods of locating graves, depending on the age of the grave:

    (i) An experienced archaeologist may recognize clues such as changes in surface contour and variation in local vegetation;

    (ii) A metal probe can be used to locate the less compact soil characteristics of grave fill;

    (iii) The area to be explored can be cleared and the top soil scraped away with a flat shovel. Graves appear darker than the surrounding ground because the darker topsoil has mixed with the lighter subsoil in the grave fill. Sometimes a light spraying of the surface with water may enhance a grave's outline;

(e) Classify the burial as follows:

    (i) Individual or commingled. A grave may contain the remains of one person buried alone, or it may contain the commingled remains of two or more persons buried either at the same time or over a period of time;

    (ii) Isolated or adjacent. An isolated grave is separate from other graves and can be excavated without concern about encroaching upon another grave. Adjacent graves, such as in a crowded cemetery, require a different excavation technique because the wall of one grave is also the wall of another grave;

    (iii) Primary or secondary. A primary grave is the grave in which the deceased is first placed. If the remains are then removed and reburied, the grave is considered to be secondary;

    (iv) Undisturbed or disturbed. An undisturbed burial is unchanged (except by natural processes) since the time of primary burial. A disturbed burial is one that has been altered by human intervention after the time of primary burial. All secondary burials are considered to be disturbed; archaeological methods can be used to detect a disturbance in a primary burial;

(f) Assign an unambiguous number to the burial. If an adequate numbering system is not already in effect, the anthropologist should devise a system;

(g) Establish a datum point, then block and map the burial site using an appropriate-sized grid and standard archaeological techniques. In some cases, it may be adequate simply to measure the depth of the grave from the surface to the skull and from the surface to the feet. Associated material can then be recorded in terms of their position relative to the skeleton;

(h) Remove the overburden of earth, screening the dirt for associated materials. Record the level (depth) and relative co-ordinates of any such findings. The type of burial, especially whether primary or secondary, influences the care and attention that needs to be given to this step. Associated materials located at a secondary burial site are unlikely to reveal the circumstances of the primary burial but may provide information on events that have occurred after that burial;

(i) Search for items such as bullets or jewellery, for which a metal detector can be useful, particularly in the levels immediately above and below the level of the remains;

(j) Circumscribe the body, when the level of the burial is located, and, when possible, open the burial pit to a minimum of 30 cm on all sides of the body;

(k) Pedestal the burial by digging on all sides to the lowest level of the body (approximately 30 cm). Also pedestal any associated artifacts;

(l) Expose the remains with the use of a soft brush or whisk broom. Do not use a brush on fabric, as it may destroy fibre evidence. Examine the soil found around the skull for hair. Place this soil in a bag for laboratory study. Patience is invaluable at this time. The remains may be fragile, and interrelationships of elements are important and may be easily disrupted. Damage can seriously reduce the amount of information available for analysis;

(m) Photograph and map the remains in situ. All photographs should include an identification number, the date, a scale and an indication of mag-netic north;

> (i) First photograph the entire burial, then focus on significant details so that their relation to the whole can be easily visualized;

> (ii) Anything that seems unusual or remarkable should be photographed at close range. Careful attention should be given to evidence of trauma or pathological change, either recent or healed;

> (iii) Photograph and map all associated materials (clothes, hair, coffin, artifacts, bullets, casings etc.). The map should include a rough sketch of the skeleton as well as any associated materials;

(n) Before displacing anything, measure the individual:

> (i) Measure the total length of the remains and record the terminal points of the measurement, e.g. apex to plantar surface of calcaneus (note: This is not a stature measurement);

(ii) If the skeleton is so fragile that it may break when lifted, measure as much as possible before removing it from the ground;

(o) Remove all elements and place them in bags or boxes, taking care to avoid damage. Number, date and initial every container;

(p) Excavate and screen the level of soil immediately under the burial. A level of "sterile" (artifact-free) soil should be located before ceasing excavation and beginning to backfill.

2. Laboratory analysis of skeletal remains

The following protocol should be followed during the laboratory analysis of the skeletal remains:

(a) Record the date, location, starting and finishing times of the skeletal analysis, and the names of all workers;

(b) Radiograph all skeletal elements before any further cleaning:

(i) Obtain bite-wing, apical and panoramic dental X-rays, if possible;

(ii) The entire skeleton should be X-rayed. Special attention should be directed to fractures, developmental anomalies and the effects of surgical procedures. Frontal sinus films should be included for identification purposes;

(c) Retain some bones in their original state; two lumbar vertebrae should be adequate. Rinse the rest of the bones clean but do not soak or scrub them. Allow the bones to dry;

(d) Lay out the entire skeleton in a systematic way:

(i) Distinguish left from right;

(ii) Inventory every bone and record on a skeletal chart;

(iii) Inventory the teeth and record on a dental chart. Note broken, carious, restored and missing teeth;

(iv) Photograph the entire skeleton in one frame. All photographs should contain an identification number and scale;

(e) If more than one individual is to be analysed, and especially if there is any chance that comparisons will be made between individuals, number every element with indelible ink before any other work is begun;

(f) Record the condition of the remains, e.g. fully intact and solid, eroding and friable, charred or cremated;

(g) Preliminary identification:

(i) Determine age, sex, race and stature;

(ii) Record the reasons for each conclusion (e.g. sex identity based on skull and femoral head);

APPENDIX E

HUMAN RIGHTS MONITORS KILLED OR DISAPPEARED IN GUATEMALA
1974 – JUNE 1991

Edmundo Guerra Theilheimer: organizer of the Committee of Relatives of the Disappeared of the University Students Association (AEU) at the University of San Carlos, shot dead at the university legal aid center by plainclothesmen on March 10, 1974.

Irma Flaquer: founder of the National Commission for Human Rights, abducted and disappeared by security forces in Guatemala City on October 16, 1980. Her 23-year-old son Fernando was killed by the security forces in the incident.

Héctor Gómez Calito: a founding member of the Mutual Support Group (GAM), abducted, tortured, and murdered on March 30, 1985.

Rosario Godoy de Cuevas: also a founding member of the GAM, Godoy was killed with her 21-year-old brother and two-year-old son on April 4, 1985. The victims were found dead inside their car at the bottom of a ravine known as a body dump near Amatitlán. Evidence, including signs that Godoy had been raped and molested and Augusto tortured before death, strongly discredited the official story that the death was accidental.

Valerio Chijal: a member of the rural Council on Ethnic Communities "We Are All Equal" (CERJ), Chijal was shot dead in the hamlet of Agostadero in the municipality of San Andrés Sajcabajá, in the department of El Quiché, on September 2, 1988. Shortly before his death, Chijal received a warning from the local civil patrol commander and military commissioners against participating in groups like the CERJ.

Pedro Cumes Pérez: a CERJ member seeking to organize a local chapter in the department of Suchitepéquez, Cumes Pérez was abducted by soldiers on the San Julián plantation and taken to the military garrison at Patulul on September 11, 1988. A writ of *habeas corpus* was filed on behalf of Pérez, but he remains disappeared.

Luis Ruiz Luis: a CERJ member who had recently participated in a CERJ rally, Ruiz was abducted with Macario Pu Chivalán from the Trinidad Miramar plantation near Patulul, Suchitepéquez, by soldiers on April 1, 1989. Several writs of habeas corpus were filed on his behalf, but he remains disappeared.

Macario Pu Chivalán: a CERJ member who had recently participated in a CERJ rally, Pu Chivalán was abducted with Luis Ruiz Luis from the Trinidad Miramar plantation near Patulul, Suchitepéquez, by soldiers on April 1, 1989. Several writs of habeas corpus were filed on his behalf, but he remains disappeared.

Nicolás Mateo: a CERJ member who had recently participated in a CERJ rally, Mateo was abducted with Agapito Pérez López from the Trinidad Miramar plantation near Patulul, Suchitepéquez, by soldiers on April 7, 1989. Several writs of habeas corpus were filed on his behalf, but he remains disappeared.

Agapito Pérez López: a CERJ member who had recently participated in a CERJ rally, Pérez was abducted with Nicolás Mateo from the Trinidad Miramar plantation near Patulul, Suchitepéquez, by soldiers on April 7, 1989. Several writs of habeas corpus were filed on his behalf, but he remains disappeared.

Aurelio Lorenzo Xicay: a GAM member kidnapped in Guatemala City on July 22, 1989, by four armed plainclothesmen with closely cropped hair, Xicay's body was found on July 24.

María Rumalda Camey: a GAM member, Camey was kidnapped by armed plainclothesmen at 5:10 a.m. on August 15, 1989, from her home in Escuintla. Although writs of habeas corpus were filed on her behalf, she remains disappeared. Later on the day that Camey was kidnapped, the Guatemala City headquarters of the GAM, where her children had sought refuge, was severely damaged by an explosive device thrown inside.

María Mejía: a member of the CERJ and the National Coordinating Body of Guatemalan Widows (CONAVIGUA), Mejía was murdered in her home in the hamlet of Parraxtut Segundo Centro, in the municipality of Sacapulas, El Quiché, by men her husband recognized as local military commissioners on March 17, 1990. Her husband, **Pedro Castro Tojín**, was also shot and left for dead.

José Vicente García: the CERJ representative from the hamlet of Chuitzalic, in the municipality of San Pedro Jocopilas, El Quiché, García was shot dead by two armed men as he walked to the hamlet La Montaña with his wife, infant son, and mother–in–law on April 10, 1990. García had been threatened by a local military commissioner because of his participation in the CERJ.

José María Ixcaya: a founding member of the CERJ, Ixcaya was shot dead by three men in civilian clothes believed to be civil patrollers as he left the hamlet of La Fe, in the village of Pujujíl, Sololá, to attend a May Day demonstration in Guatemala City. The perpetrators are believed to have acted at the behest of the civil patrol chief in a nearby hamlet, who had threatened to kill him on several occasions.

Luis Miguel Solís Pajarito: a leader of the Consejo Nacional de Desplazados (CONDEG), Solís Pajarito disappeared on May 3, 1990, after leaving the CONDEG office. Days before, he had suffered an apparent abduction attempt and had subsequently been followed. CONDEG was formed in 1989 to defend the rights of Guatemala's internally displaced population. Solís Pajarito's wife, Rosa Pu Gómez, is a member of the GAM.

Pedro Tiu Cac: a CERJ member from the Chajab area of the hamlet of Racaná, Santa María Chiquimula, in the department of Totonicapán, Tiu Cac was kidnapped by a group of about ten armed plainclothesmen, who reportedly identified themselves as investigations police (*judiciales*), at about 8:00 a.m. on July 2, 1990. On July 4, Tiu Cac was found dead, reportedly with signs of blows and bullet wounds, in the hamlet Chicox, San Francisco El Alto, Totonicapán. On October 2, 1990, a group of plainclothesmen abducted **José Pedro Tiu Chivalán**, son of Pedro Tiu Cac, from his home in Chajab as he was eating dinner with his wife and four young children. His body was found on October 5, 1990. Weeks before he was slain, Tiu Chivalán had allowed his house to be used for a meeting of a widows' rights group, CONAVIGUA. Shortly thereafter, local military commissioners came to the house and interrogated family members about the meeting. In both the case of Pedro Tiu Cac and José Pedro Tiu Chivalán, writs of habeas corpus were filed after their kidnappings to no avail.

Samuel de la Cruz Gómez: At about 3:00 a.m. on July 12, 1990, a group of about seventeen armed men kidnapped Samuel and his younger brother Genaro from their home in the village of Chimatzatz, in the municipality of Zacualpa, El Quiché, and took them away on foot. After about twenty minutes, the men freed Genaro. A group of neighbors pursued the kidnappers for several hours. At about 7:00 a.m., the kidnappers fired on the neighbors, wounding two. The neighbors later saw the kidnappers meet up with army soldiers. A writ of habeas corpus has been filed, but Samuel de la Cruz Gómez remains disappeared.

Myrna Mack: an anthropologist, founding member of the Association for the Advancement of the Social Sciences in Guatemala (AVANCSO), and consultant for the Inter-American Institute of Human Rights, Myrna Mack was stabbed to death upon leaving the AVANCSO office in Guatemala City on September 11, 1990. Mack was Guatemala's foremost researcher on the condition of the internally displaced population in the departments of El Quiché and Alta Verapaz, and a tireless advocate of the rights of this marginalized population.

Sebastián Velásquez Mejía: On October 6, the CERJ delegate in the village of Chunimá, in the municipality of Chichicastenango, El Quiché, was kidnapped from kilometer 110 of the Pan American Highway by a group of men driving a blue pickup truck which reportedly belongs to the army. The local civil patrol chief was seen indicating Velásquez's whereabouts to one of the kidnappers moments before he was captured. Velásquez was found dead in Guatemala City on October 8, 1990.

Mateo Sarat Ixcoy: A CERJ member from the hamlet of San Pedro, in the municipality of San Pedro Jocopilas, El Quiché, Sarat Ixcoy was found dead in the hamlet of La Montaña on October 29, 1990. The body was nearly decapitated and showed multiple stab wounds. Circumstantial evidence suggests that Sarat Ixcoy, like his brother-in-law, José Vicente García, was killed by local civil patrol chiefs.

Diego Ic Suy: a GAM member from Chunimá, Ic Suy was shot dead by masked men in the Zone 4 bus terminal in Guatemala City on December 10, 1990. He had complained of surveillance by the patrol chiefs of Chunimá before his death.

Juan Perebal Xirúm: a CERJ member from Chunimá, Perebal Xirúm was shot dead by six gunmen as he walked with two sons towards Chupol on February 17, 1991. One of his sons also died in the attack; the other was left paralyzed. Members of his family had been threatened repeatedly by the local civil patrol chiefs. Diego Perebal León, the son who survived, identified two of the gunmen as the local civil patrol chiefs.

Manuel Perebal Morales: a CERJ member from Chunimá, Perebal Morales was shot dead in the same incident described above.

Camilo Ajquí Jimón: a CERJ member from Potrero Viejo, in the municipality of Zacualpa, El Quiché, Ajquí Jimón was stabbed to death by three unidentified men who dragged him from his house at about 8:30 p.m. on April 14, 1991. Civil patrol chiefs and military commissioners in Potrero Viejo have repeatedly threatened to kill CERJ members in the community.

Santos Toj Reynoso: a participant in many CERJ activities along with his uncle, a CERJ member, Santos Toj Reynoso was abducted by unidentified men in Guatemala City on May 26, 1991. A body whose clothes and physical appearance reportedly matched that of Toj Reynoso was found in a dump on the outskirts of the city three days later. On May 6, 1991, civil patrollers had expelled Toj Reynoso and his uncle from their village, Cruzché IV, in the municipality of Santa Cruz del Quiché, because of their human rights activism.

Celestino Julaj Vicente: a 29–year–old CERJ delegate from Chuitzalic, in the municipality of San Pedro Jocopilas, El Quiché, Celestino Julaj Vicente was shot dead by a gunman dressed in olive green as he walked home from a festival in San Pedro Jocopilas at 11:30 p.m. on June 28, 1991. About six weeks before the murder, the civil patrol chiefs of San Pedro Jocopilas had reportedly vowed in a meeting to kill any CERJ members who attended the June 28 festival.

Americas Watch

Americas Watch was established in 1981 to monitor and promote the observance of internationally recognized human rights. Americas Watch is one of the five regional Committees of Human Rights Watch.

The Chair of Americas Watch is Peter D. Bell; Vice Chairs, Stephen L. Kass and Marina Pinto Kaufman; Executive Director, Juan E. Méndez; Associate Directors, Cynthia Arnson and Anne Manuel; Director of San Salvador Office, David Holiday; Representative in Santiago, Cynthia Brown; Representative in Buenos Aires, Patricia Pittman; Research Associate, Mary Jane Camejo; Associates, Clifford C. Rohde and Patricia Sinay.

Human Rights Watch is composed of the five Watch Committees -- Africa Watch, Americas Watch, Asia Watch, Helsinki Watch and Middle East Watch -- and the Fund for Free Expression.

Executive Committee: Chair, Robert L. Bernstein; Vice Chair, Adrian W. DeWind; Members: Roland Algrant; Lisa Anderson; Peter D. Bell; Alice L. Brown; William Carmichael; Dorothy Cullman; Irene Diamond; Jonathan Fanton; Jack Greenberg; Alice H. Henkin; Stephen L. Kass; Marina Pinto Kaufman; Jeri Laber; Aryeh Neier; Bruce Rabb; Kenneth Roth; Orville Schell; Gary G. Sick; Sophie C. Silberberg; Robert Wedgeworth.

Staff: Executive Director, Aryeh Neier; Deputy Director, Kenneth Roth; Washington Director, Holly J. Burkhalter; California Director, Ellen Lutz; Press Director, Susan Osnos; Counsel, Jemera Rone; Women's Rights Project Director, Dorothy Q. Thomas; Prison Project Director, Joanna Weschler; Managing Director, Hamilton Fish; Operations Director, Stephanie Steele; Special Events Director, Rachel Weintraub; Research Associate, Allyson Collins; Orville Schell Fellows, Robert Kushen and Dinah PoKempner.

Executive Directors

Africa Watch	Americas Watch	Asia Watch
Rakiya Omaar	Juan E. Méndez	Sidney Jones
Helsinki Watch	Middle East Watch	Fund for Free Expression
Jeri Laber	Andrew Whitley	Gara LaMarche

Physicians for Human Rights

Physicians for Human Rights (PHR) is a national organization of health professionals whose goal is to bring the skills of the medical profession to the protection of human rights. PHR work to :

* prevent the participation of doctors in torture, other serious abuses or administration of the death penalty;

* defend imprisoned health professional;

* stop physical and psychological abuse of citizens by governments; and

* provide medical and humanitarian aid to victims of repression.

Since its founding in 1986, PHR has conducted over thirty-five missions concerning twenty-three countries: Brazil, Burma, Cambodia, Chile China, Czechoslovakia, Egypt, El Salvador, Guatemala, Haiti, Iran, Iraq, Israel, and the Occupied Territories, Kenya, Kuwait, Panama, Paraguay, the Republic of Korea, Sudan, Turkey, the United States, the USSR and Yugoslavia.

PHR adheres to a policy of strict impartiality and is concerned with the medical consequences of human rights abuses regardless of the ideology of the offending government or group.